Green

Chile

Bible

Green Chile Bible

Award-Winning
New Mexico Recipes

Compiled & Edited by
The Albuquerque Tribune

Clear Light Publishing
Santa Fe, New Mexico

Clear Light Publishing
823 Don Diego
Santa Fe, New Mexico 87505
WEB: www.clearlightbooks.com

Library of Congress Cataloging-in-Publication Data

The Green chile bible : award winning New Mexico recipes / compiled and edited by *Albuquerque Tribune*
                p. cm.
      ISBN 0-940666-35-9
        1. Chili con carne. 2. Cookery—Competitions—New Mexico.
        3. Cookery—New mexico.
TX749. G823 1993   93-25576
641.8'23-dc20   CIP

First Edition
19 18 17 16 15 14 13 12 11

Printed in the U.S.A.

Acknowledgments

First, we must recognize the dozens of cooks who contributed the recipes in this book. Their hours of hard work in the kitchen have paid off in thousands of meals that have been enjoyed by many.

Then, we'd like to acknowledge former *Tribune* Editor Ralph Looney, and former features writers Lynn B. Villella and Patricia Gins, who put the original Great Green Chile Cooking Classic contest together. This book was born from the hard work they did on that contest.

Their work is linked to the present *Tribune* staff by the contributions of Ollie Reed, features writer, and Louise Lefkovitz, assistant to the editor.

We are also indebted to the New Mexico Department of Agriculture and Jeanne Croft for information and additional recipes.

Finally, we'd like to recognize our good friends at Clear Light Publisher—Marcia Keegan and Harmon Houghton. In the newspaper business, we tend to concentrate only on publishing that day's edition. It was Marcia and Harmon's vision and hard work that brought the *Green Chile Bible* to life.

Tim Gallagher, Editor
Albuquerque Tribune

Contents

Tips, Facts, and Fancies

Chile Colonizes the U.S.—Chile dishes are now eaten in every region of the United States and their popularity is rising steadily.

Chiles Everywhere—Devotees not only eat chile at home and at fine restaurants and fast food establishments, but celebrate it with everything from cookoffs and festivals to T-shirts, postcards, Christmas tree lights, earrings, and coffee cups.

Chiles by the Ton—The production of hot chiles has doubled in the United States in the past ten years. New Mexico, which plants more than 20,000 acres in chile peppers every year, produces over half the hot chiles grown in the United States.

Rainbow Varieties—Dozens of chile varieties—which ripen to red, yellow, white, orange, purple, dark brown—are grown all over the world.

Fruit or Vegetable?—The chile, although technically a fruit, has been designated New Mexico's state vegetable, along with the pinto bean. Like the tomato and potato, the chile pepper is a member of the nightshade family.

New Mexico Green—In New Mexico the chile pod in its green un-ripened state takes highest honors. The odds-on favorite is the type known as the New Mexican long green chili—or, to horticulturists, "New Mexico No. 6-4." It has a mellow distinctive flavor and ranks as medium hot.

The Jalapeño—The most famous green chile pepper in the United States. A great favorite for homemade and commercial salsas, picante sauces, and snack food toppings.

Chile Capitol of the World—That's Hatch, New Mexico, a small town in the rich southern Rio Grande valley near Las Cruces. For most New Mexicans, Hatch chiles are THE chiles.

Chile Cookoff—Chile cookery gets serious in mid-October, when candidates from all over the state meet for the New Mexico State Chile Championship cookoff in Las Cruces.

Green Chile Pizza? Quiche? Stroganoff?—Chile goes international even in New Mexico competitions—creativity know no limits.

Where the Heat Comes From—Chile's heat is concentrated in the "placenta" or central part of the pod, which produces the seeds. Heat comes from an alkaloid called capsaicin, which irritates cells lining the mouth, nose, and stomach.

Are We Addicted?—The cells exposed to capsaicin build up a tolerance to heat. At the same time they send a signal to the brain to produce morphine-like endorphins—and a natural high. Scientific studies indicate that chile is indeed addictive. Dyed-in-the-wool chile eaters literally can't get enough of it.

The Total Chile Experience—Chile stimulates the appetite, dilates blood vessels, and (eventually) cools the body. Chile temporarily speeds up the metabolism. Serious chile eaters may be more aware of other aspects of the experience—watery eyes and runny nose, flushing and sweating in the head and neck.

Vitamin C—Like all green peppers, green chiles contain large amounts of this vitamin when raw, moderate amounts after cooking. The later they are harvested, the higher the vitamin C content.

A Cure-All?—Pueblo Indians and early Spanish settlers in New Mexico prized chile as a natural digestive, herbal medicine, and disinfectant for wounds. Treatment with capsaicin (the heat-producing-chemical in chile) has given relief in ailments ranging from arthritis and shingles to acne, alcoholism, seasickness, toothaches, and ulcers. (Moderation in the use of chile is advised, however, since it is also reputed to aggravate some of those same conditions if taken in excess!)

Chile Forebears—"Chile" in Spanish, or "chili" in Mexican Nahuatl, was cultivated as early as 4000 B.C. by the Indians of the Andean highlands and was gathered for food much earlier—at least 10,000 years ago. In 1493, Columbus brought a chile pepper back to Europe, and in the sixteenth century, Spanish explorers found chile being cultivated in New Mexico.

Not an Aphrodisiac—In the sixteenth century, Jesuit priests warned the young against eating chiles, falsely believing they inspired lust.

Chile or Chili?—New Mexico has adopted "chile" officially. Some people prefer to use "chile" for the pod itself, and "chili" in recipe titles like "Chili con Carne." Peru and other South American countries avoid the chile-chili controversy by calling it "aji," pronounced "ah-hee"—similar to the sound one might make after biting into a very hot pepper for the first time.

Chile Wild and Tame—Most wild chiles grew the way nature intended them to—as colorful upright pods that attracted birds, which ate them whole and spread the seeds in their droppings. Many modern cultivated varieties have been developed to thwart hungry birds by producing drooping pods that hang inconspicuously among the leave until harvest time.

Roasting Chiles—The roasting, peeling, and freezing of green chile to be used throughout the year has become a ritual in New Mexico. In front of supermarkets, gas-fired roasters tumble the green pods in wire cages, in a few minutes providing customers with 40-pound sacks of chiles and filling the air with an unmistakable aroma that signals the end of summer. (See also "Preparing Fresh Green Chiles," page 159).

Taste Test—Cooks who are inexperienced with chile are warned to taste before adding the full amount to any dish—chile does not always comply with human hotness scales. Canned chile may also vary.

Hot to the Touch—A caution in handling chiles: wear rubber gloves.

Cooling the Chile—If chile proves too hot for your palate or your recipe, serve a side dish of sour cream with the meal. If any of your guests experiences extreme distress, offer a glass of milk (the most effective remedy)—not water, which will only make matters worse. A few bites of bread or tortilla also helps.

Breakfasts

Chile Breakfast Whirls

4 cups biscuit mix
1/2 cup margarine, melted
1 cup milk

1 lb. hot pork sausage
1 lb. regular pork sausage
1 1/2 cups green chiles, chopped

Mix the biscuit mix, margarine, and milk well; refrigerate 1/2 hour.

Meanwhile, mix the sausages and green chiles and let stand to room temperature.

Divide the dough in half. Roll out each piece to a large rectangle about 1/4 inch thick. Spread half of the sausage mixture completely over each piece of dough; roll up as for a jelly roll. Wrap in plastic wrap and freeze for 1 hour.

Remove from freezer and slice 1/3 inch thick. Freeze until ready to use. Then place the frozen slices on a cookie sheet and bake in pre-heated 400-degree oven for 20 minutes.

This is the perfect accompaniment to breakfast eggs, and it also makes a terrific appetizer.

Makes 50 to 60.

Huevos y Chilaquiles

1/2 cup onion, minced
1/3 cup butter
4 tortillas, cut into 1-inch squares
1/4 cup mild chile powder
8 eggs, slightly beaten

1/2 cup green chiles, chopped
Salt and pepper to taste
1/4 cup Parmesan cheese, grated
2 Tbs. parsley, chopped

Sauté the onion in heated butter. Add the tortillas and chile powder, stirring well to coat the tortillas with powder. Cook until browned.

Add the eggs, green chiles, salt, and pepper; scramble.

Sprinkle with the Parmesan cheese and parsley.

Serves 4.

Chiles con Huevos

1 Tbs. butter	1 Tbs. dried parsley
1 clove garlic, finely minced	1/2 tsp. oregano
1/4 lb. smoked ham, diced	6 large eggs
1/2 lb. fresh mushrooms, diced	Salt and pepper to taste
1 cup green chiles, diced	3/4 cup cheddar cheese, grated
1 cup sour cream	Olives, sliced

Preheat oven to 350 degrees.

Melt the butter in a skillet and sauté the garlic and ham for 2 minutes. Add the mushrooms and green chiles and sauté 2 more minutes.

Remove from the heat and stir in the sour cream, parsley, and oregano. Allow the mixture to stand for 10 minutes to blend flavors; then turn it into a buttered 1-quart casserole.

With a mixing spoon, make 6 rounded hollows in the chile mixture; break an egg into each hollow. Season with salt and pepper.

Bake about 20 minutes or until the egg whites are set. Sprinkle the grated cheese over the casserole and return it to the oven until the cheese is bubbling and the yolks are set, about 5 to 10 minutes more. Garnish with olive slices.

Serves 6.

Huevos Yucatecos

2 bananas
2 Tbs. butter
8 tortillas
Oil for frying
8 eggs

1 cup refried beans, warmed
1 cup cooked ham, chopped
$1/3$ cup Parmesan cheese,
  grated
$2/3$ cup peas, cooked

SAUCE:

3 Tbs. onion, chopped
2 garlic cloves, chopped
$1/4$ cup olive oil
3 tomatoes, peeled and
  chopped
1 cup tomato sauce

$1/2$ cup canned green chiles,
  chopped
$1/2$ tsp. sugar
$1/2$ tsp. vinegar
1 bay leaf
1 cup chicken broth

Sauce: Sauté the onion and garlic in hot oil. Stir in the tomatoes and tomato sauce. Fry for 5 minutes. Add the remaining sauce ingredients; simmer 5 minutes.

Slice the bananas lengthwise, then in halves; fry them in butter until browned.

Fry the tortillas in hot oil. Drain on paper towels. Then fry the eggs according to taste.

Place 2 tortillas on a plate, spread with beans, and top with 2 eggs, ham, and peas. Pour the sauce over all, sprinkle with the Parmesan cheese, and garnish with fried bananas.

Serves 4.

"I Can't Stand Eggs"

Preheat oven to 350 degrees.

Butter custard cups and break an egg into each. Add 2 tablespoons green chile sauce or salsa and top with a small slice of cheese.

Place cups in a pan of hot water and bake until eggs are set.

𝄌 𝄌 𝄌

Baked Eggs with Cheese and Chile

6 eggs
1/2 cup milk
1/2 cup cheddar cheese, grated

1 can (4 oz.) green chiles, chopped
Salt and pepper to taste

Preheat oven to 325 degrees.

Whirl the eggs, milk, and cheese in a blender until mixed. Add the green chiles, salt, and pepper and pour into a buttered 9-inch square baking dish. Bake for 25 minutes. Great for brunch or lunch or cold as an appetizer.

Serves 4 to 6.

Angi's Potluck Eggs

6 eggs
2 Tbs. milk
1/2 cup Spam, ham, or bacon,
   chopped

1/2 cup green chiles, chopped
1 can condensed cream of
   potato soup
1 Tbs. onion, chopped
Salt and pepper to taste

Beat the eggs and milk together and pour into a heated skillet. Add the remaining ingredients and stir to blend. Cook until the eggs are set. Serve over white flour tortillas or toast.

Serves 5 or 6.

Variation—Substitute cream of mushroom soup or cheddar cheese soup for cream of potato soup.

Mexican Omelet

3/4 cup avocado, chopped
1/4 cup sour cream
2 Tbs. green chiles, chopped
1 Tbs. green onion, chopped
1 tsp. lemon juice
1/4 tsp. salt
Dash hot pepper sauce

2 Tbs. butter or margarine
1 corn tortilla, torn into
   pieces
6 beaten eggs
1 cup (4 oz.) Monterey
   Jack cheese, shredded

Preheat oven to 325 degrees.

Combine the avocado, sour cream, chiles, onion, lemon juice, salt, and pepper sauce; set aside.

In a 10-inch ovenproof skillet, melt the butter; add the torn tortilla pieces and cook until soft. Pour in the eggs and cook 3 to 5 minutes. Remove from the heat and sprinkle with cheese.

Bake 3 to 4 minutes or until the cheese melts. Remove from the oven and spread the avocado mixture over half the omelet. Return to the oven for 5 more minutes. Fold the omelet in half.

Serves 4 to 6.

Chil-Ome

4 oz. bacon, finely diced
6 oz. creamed-style corn
1 can (4 oz.) green chiles,
    chopped
1 tsp. sugar
$1/8$ tsp. garlic powder

Pinch of salt
3 Tbs. light cream
8 large eggs
Salt to taste
1 cup mild cheddar cheese,
    grated

Preheat oven to 375 degrees.

Butter an 8-inch square baking dish. Fry the bacon until almost done and drain off the excess grease. Mix the bacon with the corn, chiles, sugar, garlic powder, and salt. Spread the mixture evenly in the baking dish.

Mix the cream, eggs, and salt to taste and pour over the chile mixture. Sprinkle the cheese on top. Place on the center rack of oven and bake for 35 to 40 minutes or until the eggs are set.

Serves 6.

Egg and Chile Omelet

5 slices bread, crusts removed
Butter or margarine
$3/4$ lb. longhorn cheese, grated
3 to 4 fresh green chiles,
    chopped

4 eggs, slightly beaten
2 cups milk
$1/2$ tsp. salt
$1/2$ tsp. dry mustard
Dash cayenne pepper

Butter the bread and cut the slices in cubes. Layer the bread cubes, grated cheese, and chopped chiles in a 9-inch square baking dish. Combine the remaining ingredients and pour over the bread cubes, cheese, and chiles. Let stand in the refrigerator overnight. Cover and bake for 1 hour at 325 degrees. Remove the cover and bake 5 minutes more or until puffy and set.

Serves 6.

Salsa para Huevos Rancheros
(Ranch-Style Sauce for Eggs)

8 slices bacon, cut into small
    pieces
1 large onion, thinly sliced
1 clove garlic, minced
4 to 6 green chiles, chopped

1 jalapeño chile, chopped
    (optional)
2 cups canned or fresh
    tomatoes, chopped
$1/2$ tsp. salt
$1/4$ tsp. black pepper

Fry the bacon pieces slowly until almost done; drain off all but 1 teaspoon fat. Add the onion and garlic and brown lightly. Add the remaining ingredients, cover, and simmer 20 minutes, stirring frequently.

Serve over fried or poached eggs placed on warmed or fried corn tortillas in a wide shallow bowl, allowing $1/2$ cup per serving.

This salsa is also good over any style egg, omelet, or bean burrito, or on *chiles rellenos*.

Serves 4 to 6.

Sunday Grits

4 cups boiling water
1 cup grits
1 tsp. salt
$1/4$ lb. butter, cut into chunks

1 roll (4 oz.) garlic cheese,
    cut into chunks
1 can (4 oz.) green chiles,
    chopped
4 eggs, beaten

Preheat oven to 350 degrees.

Add the grits and salt to the boiling water; cover and cook 3 to 5 minutes or until the mixture becomes thick, stirring occasionally. Remove from the heat and stir in the butter and garlic cheese. Cook, stirring, until the cheese and butter melt. Stir in the green chiles; fold in the eggs. Pour the mixture into a buttered casserole dish. Bake for 20 minutes.

Serves 8 to 10.

Chile-Cheese-Sausage Pancakes or Waffles

Pancake or waffle mix to
 serve 6
3/4 lb. bulk sausage
1 cup green chiles, chopped
1 can condensed cheddar
 cheese soup

1/4 cup milk
1/4 tsp. cumin
1/4 tsp. oregano
1/4 tsp. thyme
1/4 tsp. salt

Prepare the pancake or waffle mix according to the package directions and set aside.

Crumble the sausage and sauté it until well done. Drain off the fat. Reserve 3 tablespoons of the sausage and mix the rest along with 1/2 cup green chiles and 1/8 teaspoon of each of the spices into the pancake or waffle mix.

Empty the soup into a pan and add the milk, remaining chiles, and remaining spices. Add the salt and stir together. Heat the mixture to boiling and simmer 2 minutes. Remove from the heat and keep warm.

Prepare either pancakes or waffles and serve them hot with the cheese-chile sauce and sprinkled with reserved sausage. Great for breakfast or dinner.

Serves 6.

Green Chile Scrambled Eggs

2 medium-size avocados,
  peeled and chopped
1 Tbs. lemon juice
4 Tbs. margarine
1 small onion, minced

6 large green chiles, chopped
5 large eggs, slightly beaten
Salt to taste
Black pepper (optional)

Sprinkle lemon juice on the chopped avocados. In a large frying pan melt the margarine and cook the onion until clear but not brown. Add the avocados and cook 2 minutes. Add the chiles and cook 2 minutes more. Add the beaten eggs, season with salt and pepper, and cook until done.

Serves 5.

Appetizers

Tomato Ice

3 cups tomato juice
2 Tbs. onion, minced
2 Tbs. green chiles, chopped
1 Tbs. lemon juice
3/4 tsp. salt

1/2 tsp. basil
1 stalk celery, finely
   chopped
2 drops hot pepper sauce
2 Tbs. parsley, minced

In a medium saucepan over medium-high heat, combine all the ingredients except the parsley and heat to boiling. Reduce the heat and simmer, covered, for 5 minutes.

Strain the mixture into an 8-inch square pan; stir in the parsley. Cover and freeze until solid.

When ready to serve, let the mixture stand at room temperature for 20 minutes, occasionally breaking it up with a spoon. Beat the mixture with an electric mixer until mushy but not melted. Spoon it into sherbet glasses or appetizer dishes. Garnish each serving with a sprig of parsley.

Serves 6.

Cheese Roll Olé

roll in tortillas

2 pkgs. (8 oz. each) cream
   cheese, at room
   temperature
1 cup sharp cheddar cheese,
   grated
1 medium avocado, mashed

1 small onion, finely minced
1/2 cup pecans, finely chopped
1 tsp. garlic powder
1 can (4 oz.) green chiles,
   chopped
Salt to taste

Blend the cheeses together. Add all the other ingredients and mix well. Divide the mixture into 2 or 3 portions and form each into a roll; or form the mixture into 1 large ball. Coat it with red chile powder, parsley, paprika, or chopped nuts. Wrap in waxed paper and refrigerate overnight. Slice and serve on crackers.

Serves 16.

Guacamole

2 or 3 ripe avocados, mashed
1 medium onion, finely
    chopped
1 medium tomato, finely
    chopped

4 oz. fresh or frozen green
    chiles, chopped
Dash Tabasco sauce
1 tsp. lemon juice
Dash garlic powder
Salt to taste

Mix all the ingredients and serve with tostados or chips. Makes $2^1/_2$ cups.

Chicken Livered Cheese 'n Chile Puffs

$^1/_4$ lb. chicken livers
1 Tbs. cooking oil
$1^1/_2$ Tbs. butter
1 Tbs. onion, minced
1 medium clove garlic,
    crushed
$^1/_3$ cup tomato, peeled and
    finely chopped
1 Tbs. chicken bouillon
$^1/_4$ tsp. sugar

$^1/_2$ tsp. salt
$^1/_8$ tsp. black pepper
$^1/_2$ pkg. (8 oz.) cream cheese,
    softened
$^1/_4$ cup mayonnaise
$1^1/_2$ Tbs. green chiles,
    chopped
$^1/_4$ tsp. horseradish
1 Tbs. parsley flakes

Preheat oven to 375 degrees.

Pat the chicken livers dry; then fry them in heated oil until brown and well cooked. Cool them and chop finely.

Heat the butter and sauté the onion and garlic until limp. Add the tomato, chicken bouillon, sugar, salt, and pepper. Cook until very soft and mushy. Remove from the heat and cool. Add the livers and stir well.

Blend the softened cream cheese with the mayonnaise. Add the chiles and horseradish and mix thoroughly. Stir in the parsley flakes.

Combine the cheese and liver mixtures and pour into a shallow 1-quart casserole. Bake, uncovered, for 15 minutes or until slightly browned. Remove from the oven and cool.

Prepare Cornmeal Puffs (see recipe on next page).

Cornmeal Puffs

$^{1}/_{2}$ cup water
$^{1}/_{4}$ cup diet margarine
$^{1}/_{2}$ cup sifted white flour
2 Tbs. cornmeal

$^{1}/_{4}$ tsp. salt
$^{1}/_{2}$ tsp. baking powder
2 large eggs
paprika

Preheat oven to 400 degrees.

Bring the water to a boil. Mix the dry ingredients together well. Add the margarine to the boiling water and stir until melted. Turn the heat to low.

Add the dry ingredients all at once, stirring vigorously. Cook until the mixture draws away from the sides of the pan as you stir.

Remove from heat and cool for 1 minute. Add the eggs, one at a time, beating well after each addition until the batter is smooth.

Drop the batter by $^{1}/_{2}$ teaspoonfuls on greased cookie sheets, $1^{1}/_{2}$ inches apart. Sprinkle each lightly with paprika. Bake for 15 minutes or until golden brown.

Allow the puffs to cool completely. Then gently slice off the top half of each puff, fill with the cooled chile-liver mixture, and replace the top. Refrigerate the puffs from 1 to 5 hours before serving.

Serves 48.

Seviche

1 lb. sea scallops,
  quartered
3/4 lime juice
1/2 cup onion, finely chopped
3 canned chiles, chopped
  (or more to taste)
1/2 tsp. salt

3 small tomatoes, peeled,
  seeded, and chopped
1/2 tsp. oregano
3 Tbs. olive oil
2 Tbs. cilantro, chopped
  (coriander)

Place the scallops in a glass or ceramic bowl and add the remaining ingredients. If you have any concern about the source or freshness of the scallops, they may be poached lightly before marinating. Refrigerate at least 4 hours, stirring occasionally, before serving.
Serves 4.

Broccoli Dip

1 pkg. (10 oz.) frozen
  chopped broccoli
2 cans condensed cream of
  chicken soup
1 clove garlic, mashed

3 cups (12 oz.) Muenster
  cheese, shredded
  (or any cheese that
  melts well)
8 large green chiles, chopped
  (or to taste)

Cook the broccoli according to the package directions. Drain well. Add the soup, garlic, cheese, and green chiles. Heat until the cheese melts. Serve warm with corn chips.
Makes 5 cups.

Picante Dip

1 can (16 oz.) tomatoes
1 onion, chopped
6 to 8 green chiles, chopped

2 pkgs. (8 oz. each) cream
    cheese, softened
$1/4$ tsp. seasoning salt

Simmer the tomatoes and onion about 20 minutes. Cool the mixture until it is only warm. Add the rest of the ingredients and mash to the desired consistency for a dip. Serve with tostados.
Serves 12 to 14

Green Chile Dip

1 carton (8 oz.) sour cream
4 oz. canned or frozen green
    chiles, chopped

1 tsp. garlic powder
1 tsp. salt

Mix all the ingredients. Serve with tortilla chips or potato chips.
Serves 10.

Avocado Dip

1 lbs. Colby cheese, grated
8 oz. canned or frozen green
    chiles, chopped
2 green onions, finely
    chopped

2 avocados, mashed
Salt and pepper
1 Tbs. olive oil
1 Tbs. vinegar

Combine all ingredients and chill.
Serves 10.

Blended Chile-Avocado Dip

6 large green chiles or
    12 small chiles
1 small onion
1 large avocado
1 medium tomato

1 pkg. (4 oz.) pimento
    cream cheese
$1/4$ tsp. ground cumin
$1/2$ tsp. salt

Roast, peel, and chop the green chiles. Cut the onion, avocado, and tomato in pieces and put in a blender with the chiles, cheese, cumin, and salt. Blend at high speed 4 or 5 minutes until well blended. Serve with corn chips, potato chips, or crackers.
    Serves 15

Garden Dip

1 pkg. (8 oz.) cream cheese,
    softened
$1/2$ cup mayonnaise
$1/2$ cup small curd cottage
    cheese
$1/2$ tsp. garlic salt

Salt to taste
2 tsp. fresh chives, finely
    chopped
4 oz. canned or frozen green
    chiles, chopped

Mix the cream cheese, mayonnaise, cottage cheese, garlic salt, and salt in a blender. Stir in the chives and green chiles. Serve with potato chips or corn chips.
    Serves 20.

California Chile Dip

1 cup sour cream
1 envelope dry onion soup mix

4 oz. canned or frozen green
chiles, chopped

Mix all the ingredients together and chill.
Serves 10.

Creamy Chile Dip

1 can condensed cream of
chicken soup
4 oz. canned or frozen green
chiles, chopped

Garlic powder and
salt to taste

Warm the soup. Add the remaining ingredients and mix well. Serve
the dip warm with tostados.
Serves 12.

Gay Divorcée Dip

1 pkg. (8 oz.) cream cheese,
softened
1 cup sour cream
4 oz. canned or frozen green
chiles, chopped

$^{1}/_{4}$ tsp. garlic salt
$^{1}/_{4}$ cup crisp, crumbled bacon
or bacon tidbits

Blend together the cream cheese and the sour cream. Fold in the
remaining ingredients and chill.
Serves 20.

Traditional Chile con Queso

1 medium onion, chopped
1 clove garlic, crushed
2 Tbs. butter or margarine
1 large tomato, finely chopped
$1/2$ cup green chiles, chopped

$1/2$ tsp. oregano
$3/4$ tsp. salt
1 lb. cheddar or American
   cheese, grated

Sauté the onion and garlic in butter until soft. Add the tomato, green chiles, and seasonings and cook over low heat or in the top of a double boiler. Stir in the cheese and cook until it melts. Serve with tortilla chips.

Variation—Add 1 $1/2$ lbs. ground beef, browned.

Variation—Omit the tomatoes and add 1 16-oz. can tomatoes with green chiles, 5 drops Tabasco sauce, 2 teaspoons flavor enhancer, and 2 tablespoons hot butter. At the last minute add $1/2$ can (5 oz.) evaporated milk or enough so that the mixture is the right consistency. Serve with corn chips or vegetables.

Serves 15 to 20.

Jiffy Chile con Queso

1 can condensed cream of
    mushroom soup
6 oz. garlic cheese

1 can (4 oz.) green chiles,
    chopped

Mix the soup and the cheese over heat until the cheese melts. Add the chiles and serve warm with chips, preferably blue corn chips.
Serves 15.

Franklin's Chile con Queso

1/2 tsp. olive oil
2 Tbs. cooking oil
7 oz. canned or frozen green
    chiles, chopped
2 rolls (6 oz. each) garlic
    cheese
15 oz. Velveeta cheese

1/4 cup onion, chopped
1/4 tsp. dry red chile flakes
Dash Mexican seasoning
Salt to taste
1/2 can (8 oz.) tomatoes,
    chopped

Pour both the oils into a saucepan and add the chiles and cut up cheeses. Add all the other ingredients except the tomatoes. Cook the mixture slowly over low heat.

When the cheese melts, add the tomatoes and continue cooking over low heat for 10 minutes.
Serves 20 to 25.

Yvonne's Chile con Queso

1 can condensed cream of
   chicken soup
2 cans condensed cream of
   mushroom soup

18 oz. jalapeño cheese
   spread, chopped
1 cup green chiles, chopped
Onion and garlic salt to taste

Combine the soups and heat them slowly. Add the chopped cheese and stir until melted. Add the remaining ingredients. Serve with chips or vegetables.

Serves 15 to 20.

𝄡 𝄡 𝄡

Mini Rellenos Tempura

$1^1/_2$ lbs. cooked chicken, cubed
8 green chiles, peeled and sliced
   crosswise into $^1/_2$-inch
   slices

4 cups vegetable oil
1 tsp. salt
1 cup water
1 cup pancake mix

Wrap the green chiles around the cubes of chicken and secure them with toothpicks. Refrigerate.

Combine the oil and salt in a deep fryer and heat until a 1-inch cube of bread browns in 40 to 60 seconds.

Meanwhile, combine the pancake mix and water and beat until smooth. Roll the chile-chicken bits in the batter; then drop them in hot oil. Cook until brown. Remove them, drain, and serve with any chile con queso or with red chile sauce, page 37.

Serves 15.

Chile con Queso Sauce

1 can (4 oz.) green chiles,
   chopped
2 Tbs. chives, minced
$1/4$ cup tomato, seeds and pulp
   removed and minced

1 can condensed cream of
   chicken soup
6 oz. processed garlic
   cheese or jalapeño
   cheese roll, cut into squares

   Place all the ingredients in the top of a double boiler. Melt them, stirring, until the mixture is smooth. Serve with chips.
   Serves 10.

Cocktail Meatballs

2 lbs. lean ground beef
2 cups herb seasoned bread
   stuffing
2 eggs
1 clove garlic, crushed

$^1/_4$ cup evaporated milk
$^1/_2$ cup canned mushrooms,
   chopped
2 tsp. salt

SAUCE:

$^1/_4$ cup butter or margarine
$^1/_2$ cup onions, chopped
2 Tbs. flour
1 can (16 oz.) tomatoes

1 cup hot water
2 cups green chiles, chopped
2 cloves garlic, chopped
1 tsp. salt

Preheat oven to 375 degrees.

Mix all the meatball ingredients together and form small balls. Place them on a cookie sheet and bake for 10 minutes.

Remove the meatballs to a deep casserole and keep warm.

To make the sauce: sauté the onions in butter or margarine until they are translucent. Add the flour and brown a bit; then add the tomatoes and mash well.

Add the hot water, green chiles, garlic, and salt. Simmer 10 to 15 minutes.

Pour the sauce over the meatballs and gently mix. Serve in a chafing dish.

Makes 80 to 85. Freezes well.

Albóndigas

3 or 4 dried green chiles
1/2 cup medium grain rice
2 lbs. ground beef
1/4 cup onion, finely chopped
2 tsp. salt
1/8 tsp garlic powder

1 tsp. coriander seed, finely
   ground
2 Tbs. flour
1 egg
1/4 cup corn oil

Break up the dried green chiles and soak them in hot water about 15 minutes. Drain and chop them.

Sauté the rice in a small amount of cooking oil until it is light brown.

Break up the ground beef and add the green chiles, rice, onion, salt, garlic powder, coriander, flour, and egg. Mix thoroughly by hand.

Shape the mixture into small meatballs, about 1 inch in size. Roll them in flour and brown them in corn oil. Drain.

Place the meatballs in a 2- or 3-quart saucepan and add water to cover (1 or 2 inches). Bring them to a boil, reduce the heat, and simmer for 1 hour.

Return the meatballs and broth to a skillet with reserved corn oil and simmer for another hour. Thicken gravy if desired.

Makes 3 dozen.

Mrs. Mondragon's Cocktail Meatballs

2 lbs. lean ground beef
1 envelope (1³/₈ oz.) dehydrated
    onion soup mix
2 eggs
¹/₂ cup milk
¹/₂ cup bread crumbs
¹/₂ tsp. garlic salt
6 to 8 large mushrooms, sliced
2 Tbs. butter or margarine

¹/₄ cup margarine
¹/₄ cup flour
1 pt. milk
1 tsp. salt
1 cup sour cream
¹/₂ to 1 cup green chiles,
    chopped
1 oz. pimentos, sliced

Preheat oven to 450 degrees.

Mix the first 6 ingredients together in a large mixing bowl until well blended. Shape the mixture into 1-inch balls. Bake them for 10 minutes.

Sauté the mushroom slices in 2 tablespoons butter. Melt ¹/₄ cup margarine in a saucepan and blend in the flour. Cook a few minutes, stir in the milk, and continue stirring constantly until thickened.

Add the salt, sour cream, mushrooms, green chiles, and pimentos, stirring to blend. Spoon the red chile sauce over the meatballs.

Serves 6.

RED CHILE SAUCE:

2 Tbs. shortening
2 Tbs. flour
¹/₄ cup red chile powder

2 cups cold chicken broth
¹/₂ tsp. salt
¹/₄ tsp. garlic powder

Melt the shortening, add the flour, and stir. Add the chile powder and continue to stir until mixed. Gradually add the chicken broth and stir until there are no lumps. Season with salt and garlic powder and simmer for 10 to 15 minutes.

Mushroom Rellenos

25 medium mushrooms,
  rinsed
6 green chiles
6 Tbs. sour cream or sour
  half-and-half

$^1/_4$ tsp. garlic salt
$^1/_4$ tsp. salt
$^1/_8$ tsp. black pepper
5 Tbs. margarine
5 Tbs. wine or sherry

Preheat oven to 325 degrees.

Remove the mushroom stems and reserve. Chop the stems and the green chiles into small pieces.

Add the sour cream, garlic salt, salt, pepper, 2 tablespoons wine, and 3 tablespoons margarine. Mix thoroughly into a smooth paste.

Stuff the mixture into the mushroom caps and mound.

Pour the remaining wine into a 12×9-inch baking dish and dot with the remaining margarine. Add the stuffed mushrooms to the pan, cover, and bake for 25 minutes.

Serves 6.

❡ ❡ ❡

Nachos

Amounts of ingredients vary depending on the number of people to be served.

To Prepare: cut corn tortillas into quarters and fry them in deep fat until crisp. Drain.

Cut small pieces of cheese and lay them on the tortilla wedges. Garnish with strips of green chiles.

Place the tortillas under the broiler until the cheese melts

Green Chile Quiche in Herb Crust

HERB CRUST:

Dough for 1 9-inch pie shell
1 clove garlic, minced

1 tsp. parsley
1 tsp. cumin powder

Add the garlic, parsley, and cumin powder to the pie crust dough. Form the dough into a shell and partially bake it at 450 degrees for 8 to 10 minutes. Cool.

FILLING:

2 Tbs. butter
1 pkg. (8 oz.) cream cheese, crumbled
1/2 cup ricotta cheese
4 eggs, beaten.

1/4 cup cream
6 to 8 chiles, roasted, peeled, and chopped
1/4 cup Romano cheese, grated

Dot the cooled pie shell with butter. Add the crumbled cream cheese and the ricotta cheese to the pie shell. Beat the eggs with the cream. Pour the mixture into the pie shell. Top with the green chiles and grated cheese. Bake at 350 degrees for 45 minutes or until browned and set.

Serves 6 to 8 as an appetizer.

Green Chile Snacks

1 pkg. (3 oz.) cream cheese, softened
1/2 cup cheddar cheese, shredded
3 to 4 Tbs. green chiles, chopped
2 Tbs. onion, finely chopped
5 drops bottled hot pepper sauce
1 can (8 oz.) refrigerated crescent rolls

In a small bowl combine all the ingredients except the crescent rolls; blend very well. Separate the crescent dough into 4 rectangles. Press out the perforations to seal each rectangle together. Spread a fourth of the cheese mixture over each rectangle. Starting at the long side, roll up each rectangle, jelly roll fashion. Then cut each roll into 10 slices and refrigerate for later use.

When ready to use, place the slices cut side down on a greased cooked sheet and bake at 400 degrees for 12 to 15 minutes or until golden brown.

Makes 40.

Green Chile Beanie Bundles

1 can (8 oz.) refrigerated crescent rolls
1 1/2 cups refried beans
1/2 cup green chiles, chopped
Salt to taste
1/3 cup longhorn cheese, grated
1/2 tsp. paprika

Preheat oven to 375 degrees.

Flatten the rolls, place them on a cookie sheet, and bake them 4 to 5 minutes or until lightly browned.

Mix the beans, chiles, and salt and spread the mixture on the wide side of each roll.

Roll each one from the wide side toward the point; fold the point over and secure it with toothpicks.

Sprinkle grated cheese and paprika on top and bake for 8 to 10 minutes or until heated through and brown.

Serves 4.

Chile-Cheese Squares

2 lbs. cheddar cheese, grated
2 cans (4 oz. each) green
   chiles, chopped

12 eggs, well beaten
Paprika

    Preheat oven to 350 degrees.
    Layer the cheese and chiles in a buttered baking dish. Pour the eggs over and dust with the paprika. Bake for 30 minutes or until it tests done. Cut into small squares and serve as an appetizer.
    Serves 8.

    Variation—Use 1 lb. cheddar cheese and 1 lb. Monterey Jack cheese. Garnish with black olives and pimento.

    Variation—Use whole green chiles to line a pie pan. Spread 1/4 lb. grated cheddar cheese over the chiles. Beat 5 eggs with 2 tablespoons cream and salt and pepper to taste. Pour the mixture over the cheese and chiles and bake as above.

Chil-E-Ums

1 large pkg. hot roll mix
1/2 lb. crisp bacon
1 medium onion

1 can (4 oz.) green chiles,
   drained and chopped

    Preheat oven to 375 degrees.
    Prepare the hot roll mix following the directions on the box. Break up the bacon, chop the onion, and mix together with the green chiles. Divide the roll mix into 48 equal parts. Using your hands, spread out each piece and fill it with 1/2 to 3/4 teaspoon of the above mixture. Pinch the rolls together and bake for 12 to 15 minutes or until golden brown.
    Makes 48.

Zesty Sausage Squares

1 cup buttermilk biscuit mix
1/3 cup milk
4 Tbs. mayonnaise
1 lb. hot pork sausage
1/2 cup onion, chopped

1 egg
2 cups cheddar cheese, grated
2 cans (4 oz. each) green
    chiles, chopped

Preheat oven to 375 degrees.

Mix the biscuit mix with the milk and 2 tablespoons mayonnaise and spread the mixture in a well-greased 9×13-inch casserole. Pat down.

Sauté the sausage and onion. Drain on paper towels; then spread on biscuit mixture.

Beat the egg with the remaining mayonnaise, cheddar cheese, and green chiles. Spread on top of the meat layer. Bake for 25 minutes.

Cut into 1-inch squares for appetizers or serve larger squares for brunch.

Makes 100 1-inch squares.

Chile-Cheese Bits

1 cup margarine
1 tsp. salt
1/2 tsp. red chile powder
1/2 lb. sharp cheddar cheese,
    grated

2 cups flour
2 cups crisp rice cereal
1 can (4 oz.) green chiles,
    drained and chopped

Preheat oven to 350 degrees.

Cut the first 5 ingredients together like pastry. Mix in the rice cereal. Form the mixture into walnut-size balls and make a dent in each ball. Place them on a slightly greased cookie sheet. Fill each thumbprint with chopped green chile. Bake for 20 minutes.

Makes 5 dozen.

Chile-Izzas

1 lb. lean ground beef
Salt to taste
2 tubes (10 oz. each)
    refrigerator biscuits

1 can (8 oz.) Spanish-style
    tomato sauce
$^1/_2$ lb. mozzarella cheese
1 or 2 cans (4 oz. each)
    green chiles, chopped

Preheat oven to 375 degrees.

Brown the ground beef and drain. Salt to taste.

Separate the biscuits and roll them out into circles. Place them on a greased cookie sheet and spread tomato sauce on them.

Add a layer of meat, then chiles; top with cheese. Bake for 15 to 20 minutes. Cut each circle into quarters and serve hot.

Makes 80.

Variation—Add sour cream or substitute pork sausage for the ground beef.

Perritos Verdes
(Green Chile Puppies)

20 cocktail franks or 1 pkg.
    (1 lb.) franks cut into
    1$^1/_2$-inch strips

1 can (10 oz.) green chile
    strips or sauce
12 corn tortillas, cut into
    1$^1/_2$-inch pieces.

Wrap the franks in strips of green chile or slice them partially through and fill the openings with green chile sauce. Wrap tortilla strips around the franks and secure them with toothpicks. Fry them briefly in hot deep fat until crisp.

Serves 6 to 8.

Chile-Cheese Puffs

2¹/₂ cups cheddar cheese, grated

1¹/₂ cups dry-curd cottage cheese

¹/₂ large onion, minced

¹/₂ tsp. salt

1 cup green chiles, chopped

2 eggs

³/₄ cup water

¹/₂ tsp. salt

³/₄ cup flour

Mix the first 5 ingredients together until well blended. Chill the mixture until firm.

Beat the eggs, water, and salt until foamy. Add the flour and mix thoroughly. Chill several hours. The batter must be thick.

Form the cheese mixture into marble-size balls. Then dip them in batter to cover them completely. Fry them in 2 inches of hot oil until golden brown. Drain.

Makes 50.

Salads

Green Chile Salad

1 Tbs. vinegar
1 Tbs. salad oil
1 clove garlic, cut
1 large tomato, diced

1 small onion, finely chopped
$^{1}/_{2}$ cup fresh green chiles,
    chopped

Combine the vinegar and salad oil. Rub a bowl with the cut garlic and add the diced tomato, onion, and green chiles. Let stand for 30 minutes. Add the vinegar and salad oil and toss gently. Serve on lettuce leaves or serve in the center of scoops of small curd cottage cheese.
Serves 4.

Marinated Garden Salad

4 tomatoes, cut into wedges
4 green chiles, roasted,
    peeled, and sliced
2 Tbs. green onions or
    chives, minced
1 lemon, thinly sliced

$^{1}/_{4}$ cup vegetable oil
2 Tbs. vinegar
$^{1}/_{4}$ tsp. salt
$^{1}/_{4}$ tsp. pepper
$^{1}/_{4}$ tsp. oregano leaves

Toss together the tomatoes, green chiles, onions, and lemon slices. Add oil, vinegar, salt, pepper, and oregano. Cover and marinate in the refrigerator at least 2 hours. At serving time, remove the lemon slices and serve the salad in lettuce cups.
Serves 8.

Cucumber Cream Salad

¹/2 cup dried onion soup mix
1 pt. sour cream
¹/4 cup lemon juice
1 tsp. sugar

3 large green chiles,
    chopped
2 medium cucumbers, thinly
    sliced and drained

In a large bowl, blend together the dried onion soup and sour cream. Add the lemon juice, sugar, green chiles, and cucumbers and toss well. Chill.
Serves 6.

Guacamole Salad

1 medium head of lettuce,
    cored and washed
2 medium tomatoes, cut into
    wedges
4 or 5 green onions, chopped
4 or 5 large green chiles
    roasted, peeled, and chopped

1 large avocado, peeled
    and sliced
1 large lemon, halved
Freshly ground black pepper
    or lemon-seasoned
    pepper

Tear the lettuce into bite-size pieces. Add the tomatoes, green onions, and green chiles. Toss lightly. Add the avocado, tossing again, and squeeze half of the lemon over the salad. Sprinkle with pepper and garnish with slices of the remaining lemon. Serve with crackers or croutons.
Serves 4.

Piquant Salad

1 pkg. (3 oz.) lime gelatin
1 cup hot water
2 green chiles, chopped

1 can (4 oz.) tomato and
    green chile sauce

Dissolve the gelatin in 1 cup hot water in an 8×10-inch pan. Set until lightly thickened and add the remaining ingredients. Chill until firm.
Serves 6.

𝄿 𝄿 𝄿

Green Chile and Cucumber Salad

1 pkg. (6 oz.) lime gelatin
1 carton (8 oz.) sour cream
2 cups peeled cucumber,
    chopped

$^1/_2$ cup green chiles, chopped
1 cup salad olives
2 Tbs. vinegar
2 Tbs. celery seed

Dissolve the gelatin according to the package directions. Stir in the remaining ingredients.
Place 12 large paper baking cups in muffin tins and spoon the gelatin mixture in. Chill until set.
Makes 12.

Molded Chile Salad

1 Tbs. gelatin
3 Tbs. cold water
1 1/2 cups clear chicken broth
3/4 tsp. salt
1/4 tsp. paprika
4 Tbs. wine vinegar
1 cup green chiles, chopped

1 green onion, chopped
3/4 cup equal parts chopped
    celery, chopped
    cucumber, grated
    carrots, chopped
    sweet red pepper, or
    pimentos

Soak the gelatin in cold water. Heat the chicken broth and dissolve the gelatin in it. Add the salt, paprika, and vinegar.

Chill until almost set. Add the remaining ingredients and chill until set.

Serves 5 to 6.

Hattie's New Mexico Christmas Salad Mold

1 pkg. (6 oz.) lemon gelatin
2 cups hot tomato juice
2 cups cold tomato juice
1 Tbs. fresh lemon juice
3 cans (4 oz. each) green
    chiles, chopped
1/2 cup chopped celery, leaves
    included
1/2 tsp. garlic salt

1/2 tsp. onion salt
Dash black pepper
Dash hot pepper sauce
1/2 tsp. Beau Monde spice
2 medium avocados, cut in
    bite-size pieces
1 cup sour cream
2 Tbs. mayonnaise

Dissolve the gelatin in boiling hot tomato juice. Add the cold tomato juice and stir. Add the lemon juice and remaining ingredients except the sour cream and mayonnaise.

Pour into a ring mold and chill until set. Turn out onto a chilled platter and garnish with curly endive and seedless grapes.

Combine the sour cream and mayonnaise and place in the center of the mold.

Serves 8 to 10.

Taco Salad

1 lb. ground beef
1 pkg. (1 1/4 oz.) taco
   seasoning mix
3/4 cup water
1 can (16 oz.) ranch-style
   beans, chilled and
   drained
1 head lettuce

2 tomatoes, diced
1 onion, finely chopped
1 can (4 oz.) green chiles,
   chopped
1 lb. cheese, grated
3/4 cup bottled French
   dressing, chilled
2 cups small corn chips,
crushed

Brown the ground beef; add the seasoning mix and water. Add the ranch-style beans and simmer; then chill the mixture for 30 minutes.

Combine the lettuce, tomatoes, onion, green chiles, cheese, and dressing. Chill.

Just before serving combine both mixtures with the crushed corn chips; mix well and serve.

Serves 8 to 10.

Variation—Use a half envelope of onion soup mix instead of the taco seasoning mix. Add 1/4 cup chopped green pepper and 1/2 cup sliced olives. Omit the dressing and beans. Combine the vegetables and spoon on the meat mixture; then top with crushed tortilla chips.

Variation—Omit the ground beef and use 2 cans of beans. Use Italian salad dressing, omit the seasoning mix, increase the onion to 2 onions, and toss the whole mixture together.

Mexican Chef's Salad

1 lb. ground beef
1 can (16 oz.) kidney beans,
    drained (optional)
1/4 tsp. salt
1 can (4 oz.) green chiles,
    chopped
1 head lettuce, torn into pieces
4 tomatoes, cut into wedges
1 red or white onion, sliced into rings

1 cucumber, peeled and sliced
2 cups tortilla chips,
    crushed
1 large avocado, peeled and
    sliced
4 oz. cheddar cheese, grated
1/2 to 1 cup Thousand Island
    dressing

Brown the beef; pour off the fat and add the drained beans, salt, and chiles. Simmer 10 minutes.

Combine the lettuce, tomatoes, onion slices, and cucumber slices in a large bowl.

Add the crushed chips, avocado slices, and cheese. Toss together. Pour the salad dressing over and toss lightly. Add the cooled beef mixture and toss again.

Decorate with more tortilla chips, avocado slices, and tomato wedges.

Serves 4 to 6

Chilemac Salad

4 cups elbow macaroni, cooked
1 cup mild cheddar cheese,
    diced
1/2 cup green chiles, diced
6 Tbs. onion, finely chopped

1 cup mayonnaise or salad
    dressing
1/2 cup sweet pickles, chopped
1/2 tsp. salt

Mix all the ingredients together. Cover and chill several hours.
Serves 8 to 10.

New Mexico Potato Salad

4 large potatoes
4 large eggs
5 green onions (green
   stalks only)

6 large green chiles
2 cups mayonnaise
Salt and pepper to taste

Boil the potatoes until firm but not soft. Hard-boil the eggs. Chop the onion and green chiles. Chop the potatoes and eggs into cubes.

Mix the potatoes, onions, eggs, and chiles in a bowl with the mayonnaise. Toss well. Salt and pepper to taste.

Serves 6.

Soups and Stews

Southwestern Corn Chowder

6 slices bacon
$^1/_2$ cup onion, chopped
1 large potato, diced
$^1/_2$ cup water
1 can (17 oz.) creamed-style
   corn
1 can condensed cream of
   mushroom soup

2 oz. mushrooms, sliced
2 cups milk
1 tsp. salt
1 can (4 oz.) green chiles,
   chopped

Cook the bacon until crisp. Drain. Pour off all but 3 tablespoons of bacon drippings. Add the onion and potato and cook over medium heat, stirring, until the onion is lightly browned.

Add water, cover, and simmer until the potato is just tender. Stir in the corn, soup, mushrooms, milk, and salt. Heat to boiling; lower the heat, add the chiles, and simmer a few minutes.

Serve in soup bowls or a tureen. Crumble bacon on top.

Serves 6.

Traditional Gazpacho

$1^1/_2$ quarts tomato juice
1 bell pepper, chopped
1 onion, chopped or
   equivalent onion powder
1 cucumber, peeled and chopped
2 to 4 tomatoes, peeled and
   chopped

Green chile to taste
2 cloves garlic, or equivalent
   garlic powder
1 to 2 Tbs. olive oil
1 Tbs. vinegar
Dash oregano
1 to 2 tsp. lemon juice

Mix all the ingredients in a bowl and chill for 6 to 8 hours. Serve with crackers or French bread.

Serves 4.

Blender Gazpacho

$^1/_2$ cup water
2 Tbs. olive oil
2 Tbs. dry red wine
$^1/_2$ tsp. salt
$^1/_4$ tsp. oregano
$^1/_4$ tsp. cumin
1 clove garlic
2 large tomatoes, quartered

1 green chile, quartered, seeds
   and veins removed
3 green onions, cut into
   1-inch pieces
2 sprigs parsley
1 medium cucumber, peeled
   and cut into 1-inch
   pieces

Measure the first 9 ingredients directly into a blender and blend for 10 to 15 seconds. Add the remaining ingredients and blend for 10 seconds or just until the onions and cucumber are coarsely chopped.

Serves 6 to 8.

Sopa de Patata Español
(Spanish Potato Soup)

4 strips bacon, cut in 1-inch
   square
4 cups potatoes, diced
2 cans (8 oz. each) tomato
   paste
2 cups green chiles, chopped
$^1/_2$ cup onion, finely chopped
2 tsp. salt

1 tsp. celery seed
1 tsp coarse black pepper
7 cups cold water
1 bay leaf
1 clove garlic, chopped
$^1/_2$ tsp. powdered cumin
Cheese, grated
Oregano

Fry the bacon squares until crisp. Drain and reserve. Roll the diced potatoes in the bacon drippings and place them in a large kettle with all ingredients except the bacon, cheese, and oregano.

Simmer for 2 hours.

To serve: place the bacon squares in the bottom of a soup tureen. Add the grated cheese and a pinch of oregano. Pour boiling soup over. Serve with tortillas.

Serves 8.

Caldo Varsoviana

1 cup clear chicken broth
1 cup raw green cabbage,
   shredded

1 can condensed cream of
   chicken soup
$^1/_2$ soup can water
1 cup green chiles, chopped

Stir the cabbage into the broth and bring to a boil; then simmer for 5 minutes.

Remove from the heat and add the condensed cream of chicken soup blended with water. Stir until smooth.

Add the green chiles and stir.

Return to the heat and simmer for 5 minutes, stirring occasionally. Serves 4.

Weight Watchers' Green Chile Soup

$1^1/_2$ cups tomato juice
2 Tbs. onion, minced
$^1/_4$ cup green chiles, chopped

$^1/_4$ canned mushrooms,
   chopped
Salt and pepper to taste
2 oz. Swiss cheese, grated

Mix all the ingredients except the cheese in a saucepan. Bring to a boil, reduce heat, and add the cheese just before serving. Simmer until the cheese melts.

Serves 1 a hearty lunch.

Avocado Soup

1 med. tomato, peeled
   seeded and chopped
4 cups chicken broth
1 Tbs. onion, minced
$^1/_2$ cup heavy cream

1 tsp. lemon juice
Salt and pepper to taste
2 large avocados
$^1/_4$ cup dry sherry

Place all ingredients, except the avocados and sherry in a blender until well blended. Heat this mixture in a saucepan and simmer for a few minutes.

Peel and mash avocados and then blend into soup. Add sherry, heat through, and serve.

This soup is also delicious served cold. For an extra touch of flavor add one or two thin slices of banana.

Serves 4 to 6.

Green Chile au Vin

1 Tbs. bacon drippings
1 lb. lean ground beef
1 medium onion, chopped
2 cans (16 oz. each) tomatoes
4 green chiles, peeled and
    chopped
$1/2$ cup dry red wine
$1/2$ cup water
1 tsp salt

$1/8$ tsp. black pepper
1 Tbs. oregano
1 Tbs. chile powder
$1/8$ tsp. cinnamon
1 Tbs. garlic powder
$1/4$ cup dry red wine
1 can (4 oz.) mushrooms,
    undrained

Brown the ground beef in the bacon drippings; add the onions and sauté until they are golden. Drain. Add the tomatoes, chiles, $1/2$ cup wine, water, salt, pepper, oregano, chile powder, cinnamon, and garlic powder. Mix well.

Simmer 30 minutes, adding more water as necessary. Add $1/4$ cup wine and mushrooms and continue simmering until the liquid is reduced but the mixture is still moist.

Serves 4.

Green Chile Stew

2 lbs. round steak, cubed
Cooking oil
$1^1/2$ large onions, chopped
1 clove garlic, minced
5 cans (10 oz. each) tomatoes
    with green chiles

2 cans (10 oz. each) whole
    green chiles, coarsely
    chopped
2 cups water
2 tsp. beef bouillon powder
    (or 2 beef bouillon cubes)

Brown the cubed round steak slowly in small amount of cooking oil; add the chopped onions and garlic and simmer for 5 minutes.

Add the remaining ingredients and simmer, covered, for 3 hours or until the meat is tender. May be refrigerated or frozen with excellent results.

Serves 8.

Variation—Add 2 cans (16 oz. each) pinto beans or 2 cans (16 oz. each) yellow hominy.

Variation—Substitute 2 lbs. lean ground round for cubed round steak.

Variation—Omit 1 can of tomatoes with green chiles and add 2 cups canned tomatoes, chopped.

Variation—For a heartier stew add 2 medium potatoes, diced, and 2 carrots, sliced.

Variation—Substitute 1 large can (46 oz.) cocktail vegetable juice for the cans of tomatoes with green chiles.

Fire Chief's Hot Stew

2 lbs. fresh green chiles, hot or mild (or 1 qt. frozen)	1 can (32 oz.) tomatoes
2 cups water	2 lbs. beef stew meat
1 clove garlic	6 large potatoes, cooked and diced
1 small onion, chopped	Longhorn cheese, grated (optional)

Roast, peel, and chop the fresh green chiles; in 2 cups of water simmer the chiles, garlic, onion, and tomatoes for 1 hour.

Pressure cook the stew meat in 1 quart water for 15 minutes (or simmer, covered, for 1 hour). Reserve the meat liquid and add it to the chile mixture. Add the diced potatoes and simmer 30 minutes longer. Spoon into serving bowls and top with grated longhorn cheese, if desired.

Serves 10.

Robust Green Chile Stew

1 lb. lean ground beef
1 lb. lean pork, cut into
    $^1/_2$ inch cubes
1 can (15 oz.) white hominy
    undrained
1 can (16 oz.) pinto beans,
    undrained
1 can (16 oz.) tomatoes,
    chopped, undrained

2 large onions, chopped
2 to 3 cloves garlic, minced
4 to 5 medium potatoes, cubed
1$^1/_2$ cups green chiles, chopped
6 beef bouillon cubes
1 tsp. cider vinegar
3 cups water
Salt to taste

Brown the beef and pork together. Drain off the fat. Add the remaining ingredients. Cover and simmer 4 to 6 hours, stirring occasionally.

Makes 4 to 5 quarts.

Minnesota Bachelor's Chile

1$^1/_2$ lbs. lean pork, cubed and
    browned
1$^1/_2$ pints vegetable juice
    cocktail
1 can (16 oz.) kidney beans
1 pkg. (1$^1/_4$ oz.) chile seasoning
    mix

2 cans (4 oz.) green chiles
    chopped
1 Tbs. ground chile powder
$^1/_2$ pkg. (6 oz.) frozen chopped
    onions

Combine all the ingredients in a heavy casserole with a tight-fitting lid. Bake at 195 degrees all day. Serve with flour tortillas.

Serves 4.

Chile con Carne de Venado
(Chile with Venison)

2 lbs. venison, cut into 1-inch
    cubes
Flour for dredging
1 large onion, chopped
$1/2$ green pepper, chopped
$1/2$ cup vegetable oil

$1^{1}/2$ cups green chiles,
    chopped
1 can (16 oz.) tomatoes
Salt to taste
$1/2$ tsp. garlic powder
1 tsp. oregano

Dredge the meat in flour and brown well. Add the onion and green pepper and cook until the onion is tender. Drain.

Add the remaining ingredients and simmer for 1 hour.

Serves 8 to 10.

Bean and Chicken Stew

$1/2$ lb. pinto beans
1 cup soybeans
2 cups cooked chicken,
    chopped
$1/2$ cup onion, finely chopped
$1/4$ cup green chiles, finely chopped

$1/2$ cup white rice, uncooked
1 tsp. garlic, minced
1 tsp prepared mustard
1 tsp. salt
2 cups chicken broth

Rinse the beans and drain. Cover the beans with water and soak them for 2 hours, adding water to keep beans covered. Cook the beans in the soaking water until soft, adding more water as necessary.

About 40 minutes before serving add the remaining ingredients and simmer. Serve with corn bread.

Serves 4 to 6.

Chile Gumbo

2 medium onion, coarsely
  chopped
2 cloves garlic, crushed
2 oz. salt pork, diced
1 can (16 oz.) tomatoes,
  chopped
1 lb. coarsely ground lean
  beef
2 cups vegetable juice cocktail
1 pkg (10 oz.) frozen cut okra
2 cans (4 oz. each) green chiles,
  chopped

1 bay leaf
1 to 2 cups water
1 can (15 oz.) black-eyed peas
  with bacon
2 Tbs. dried parsley flakes
Salt to taste
1 Tbs. chile powder
  (optional)
1 Tbs. filé powder
4 cups cooked rice

Sauté the onions and garlic with the salt pork until limp. Add the chopped tomatoes with their juice. Sauté 10 minutes more.

Add the beef, stirring until it is browned. Add the vegetable juice, okra, green chiles, and bay leaf. Cook over medium heat 45 to 60 minutes, adding water if necessary.

Then add the black-eyed peas, parsley, and more water to maintain a soup-like consistency. Cook 30 minutes more, stirring occasionally. Add the salt and chile powder. Cook 10 minutes more. Stir in the filé powder and cook 3 to 5 minutes only. Filé powder loses its effect if reheated. Serve in large bowls or with rice.

Serves 8.

Vegetables

Southwest Baked Beans

4 cans (16 oz. each) pinto
   beans, drained
1/2 cup sorghum
1/2 cup catsup
2 small onions, chopped
1 tsp. garlic salt

1 can (4 oz.) green
   chiles, chopped
1 tsp. prepared mustard
1 can (10 oz.) tomatoes
   with green chiles
2 slices bacon

Preheat oven to 400 degrees.

In a large mixing bowl, combine all the ingredients except the bacon; mix thoroughly. Pour into a 2- or 3-quart ovenproof casserole or bean pot. Top with the bacon cut in 1-inch pieces. Bake for 1 1/2 hours.

Serves 8 to 10.

Broccoli-Green Chile Delight

2/3 cup onion, diced
2/3 cup celery, diced
2 Tbs. cooking oil
1 pkg. (10 oz.) frozen chopped
   broccoli, thawed
1 can condensed cream of
   mushroom soup

1/2 soup can milk
1 cup water
1 cup instant rice, uncooked
1 jar (8 oz.) processed cheese
   spread
1 cup green chiles,
   chopped

Preheat oven to 350 degrees.

Sauté the onion and celery in oil; add the thawed broccoli. Simmer over low heat 15 minutes. Add the soup, milk, water, rice, cheese spread, and chiles; bring the mixture to a boil.

Pour into a buttered 1 1/2-quart casserole. Bake for 25 minutes or until well heated.

Serves 6.

Cauliflower-Chile Soufflé

2 lbs. cauliflower, fresh or
    frozen
1 tsp. butter
1/4 cup wheat germ
1/4 cup light cream or milk
4 egg yolks, beaten

5 to 7 green chiles, peeled and
    chopped
1/4 cup onion, finely chopped
1/2 tsp. salt
4 egg whites, stiffly beaten
Wheat germ
1/2 cup cheese, grated

Preheat oven to 350 degrees.

Clean and cook the cauliflower until tender. Mash the cauliflower into a smooth paste. Add the butter, 1/4 cup wheat germ, cream, egg yolks, chiles, onion, and salt. Blend well.

Fold in the egg whites.

Pour the mixture into a buttered 2-quart casserole. Sprinkle with a small amount of wheat germ. Top with the grated cheese. Bake for 25 to 30 minutes.

Serves 6 to 8.

Creamy Corn Casserole

1 can (12 oz.) creamed-style
    corn
1 cup cracker crumbs, crushed
1/2 cup celery, finely chopped
1/2 cup onion, finely chopped
1 cup cheddar cheese, grated

1 tsp. salt
2 eggs, beaten
1 cup milk
2 Tbs. margarine
1 can (4 oz.) green chiles,
    chopped

Preheat oven to 350 degrees.

Combine all the ingredients and pour into a greased 1 1/2-quart casserole. Bake 50 minutes.

Serves 6 to 8.

Curried Corn with Chile

$^1/_2$ cup butter
1 clove garlic, finely minced
1 medium onion, chopped
8 ears corn
1 Tbs. curry powder

Salt and freshly ground black
   pepper to taste
1 cup heavy cream
1 can (4 oz.) green chiles,
   chopped

Melt the butter in a heavy skillet and add the garlic and onion. Cook until the onion is translucent.

Using a sharp knife, cut the corn kernels off the cobs; then scrape the cobs to remove the corn milk. Add the kernels and corn milk to the skillet.

Sprinkle with the curry powder, salt, and pepper; add the cream. Partially cover and simmer 20 to 30 minutes over very low heat. Stir in the chiles, cook 3 minutes longer, and serve.

Serves 6.

Cornfetti Casserole

1 can (16 $^1/_2$ oz.) cream-style
   yellow corn
1 can (4 oz.) green chiles,
   chopped
$^1/_2$ cup yellow cornmeal
1 tsp. baking powder

$^1/_2$ tsp. salt
2 eggs, beaten
1 cup milk
1 cup cheese, grated
1 tsp. sugar
$^1/_2$ cup onion, finely
   chopped

Preheat oven to 350 degrees.

Mix together all the ingredients except the cheese and chiles and layer the cornmeal mixture with chiles in a greased 2-quart casserole.

Top with the grated cheese. Bake for 1 hour or until set.

Serves 6 to 8.

Variation—Add 1 cup sour cream and 1 jar (2 oz.) chopped pimentos to the mixture.

Corn and Green Chile

3 cups fresh corn, cut
   from the cob
3 Tbs. cooking oil
2 to 4 green chiles

1 clove garlic, finely chopped
$^3/_4$ tsp. salt
$^1/_8$ tsp. pepper

    Heat the oil in a skillet and add the corn, chiles, and garlic. Cover and cook slowly until the corn is tender, 10 to 15 minutes.
    Add the seasonings. If the corn is too dry, add several tablespoons of boiling water while cooking.
    Serves 6.

Eggplant Olé

1 large eggplant, pared and
   cut into $^1/_2$-inch slices
6-8 whole green chiles, cut
   in strips
1 cup butter, melted

1 cup cornflake crumbs
$^1/_2$ tsp. salt
1 can (10 oz.) green chile
   enchilada sauce
2 cups longhorn cheese,
   grated

    Preheat oven to 450 degrees.
    Grease two pizza pans. Dip the eggplant slices in butter, then in cornflake crumbs; sprinkle with salt. Place the slices on pans and cover each slice with strips of green chile. Spoon enchilada sauce over each slice and generously sprinkle with grated cheese. Bake 15 minutes. Freezes well.
    Serves 6.

Green Beans with Green Chile

1 lb. green beans	2 green chiles, chopped
3 Tbs. vegetable oil	1 cup chicken or beef broth
2 Tbs. onion, minced	1/4 tsp. salt
1 can (8 oz.) tomato sauce	Oregano, crushed

String, wash, and cut the beans in half lengthwise. Wilt the onion in hot oil; add the tomato sauce, chiles, string beans, broth, and salt. Cover tightly and cook just until the beans are tender. Garnish with crushed oregano.

Serves 4.

Green Beans Supreme

1 can condensed cream of mushroom soup	1 cup sharp cheddar cheese, shredded
3 pkgs. (1 lb. each) frozen French-style green beans	1/4 tsp. garlic salt
4 Tbs. milk	1 pkg. (10 oz.) frozen French-fried onion
1 can (4 oz.) green chiles, chopped	rings

Preheat oven to 350 degrees.

Combine all the ingredients except the onion rings in a greased casserole. Stir lightly to blend well.

Bake for 25 minutes. Remove from oven and layer the onion rings on top. Return to the oven and bake 10 minutes longer.

Serves 8.

Hominy and Green Chile Casserole

2 cans (15 oz. each) golden
   hominy
1 can (4 oz.) green chiles
$^1/_4$ cup parsley, chopped

$^1/_4$ cup onion, finely chopped
$^1/_2$ cup sour cream
$^1/_4$ to $^1/_2$ tsp. chile powder
$^3/_4$ cup cheddar cheese,
   grated

Preheat oven to 350 degrees.

Drain the hominy. Layer half of the green chiles in a 1-quart greased casserole. Add the hominy and top with the remaining green chiles. Mix the parsley, onion, sour cream, and chile powder together and pour over the layers.

Top with the grated cheese. Bake, covered, for 30 minutes.

Serves 4.

Variation—Substitute 1 can of condensed cheddar cheese soup for the sour cream and mix all the ingredients together instead of layering.

Variation—Mix 3 or 4 tablespoons melted butter into the casserole along with 1 jar (3 oz.) chopped pimentos.

New Mexico Caviar

5 cups cooked dry black-eyed
   peas
$^1/_2$ cup olive oil
$^1/_4$ cup plus 2 Tbs. vinegar
1 tsp. garlic juice
$^1/_2$ cup onions, thinly sliced
   and quartered

3/4 tsp. salt
$^1/_2$ tsp. freshly ground black
   pepper
4 oz. canned or frozen green
   chiles, chopped

Drain the peas well and mash them slightly. Add the remaining ingredients and stir well.

Refrigerate for 3 days. Serve on a bed of shredded lettuce as an hors d'oeuvre or serve as a side dish.

Serves 10.

Garbanzos Calientes

3 Tbs. oil
1 onion, finely chopped
1 clove garlic, finely chopped
$1/4$ tsp. oregano
1 tomato, peeled and chopped

2 canned green chiles,
   chopped (or more
   to taste)
2 tsp. red chile powder
1 can (16 oz.) garbanzos
   chickpeas), drained
Salt to taste

Heat the oil in a skillet and sauté the onion, garlic, oregano, tomato, chiles, and chile powder over low heat about 10 minutes.

Add the garbanzos and salt; simmer 20 minutes.

Serves 4.

Mexicali Spuds

4 strips bacon
5 medium potatoes, cubed
2 Tbs. cream
1 pt. sour cream
1 can (4 oz.) green chiles,
   chopped

6 green onions, sliced
Salt
Pepper
Garlic salt

Fry the bacon, drain on paper towels, and crumble. Cook the potatoes in salted boiling water until tender; drain and cool for 45 minutes.

Mix together the crumbled bacon, cream, sour cream, green chiles, and onions. Fold into the potatoes and season to taste with salt, pepper, and garlic salt. Can be served immediately or can be chilled.

Serves 6.

Foil-Baked Chile Potatoes

3 large potatoes, pared and
    sliced
Salt
Pepper
4 slices bacon, fried and
    crumbled
1 medium onion, sliced

8 oz. sharp cheddar cheese,
    grated
3 green chiles, peeled and
    chopped
$1/2$ cup margarine

Preheat oven to 350 degrees.

Arrange the sliced potatoes on a large section of aluminum foil and sprinkle with salt and pepper. Crumble the bacon over top and then spread with the onion, cheese, and chiles. Dot with pats of margarine.

Fold up the edges of the foil and seal tightly, leaving room for steam. Bake for 1 hour.

Serves 6.

(This recipe is ideal for outdoor cooking. If using an outdoor charcoal grill, seal the potato jacket in an extra layer of foil.)

Chile Scalloped Potatoes

6 to 8 large potatoes, thinly
    sliced
4 green chiles, roasted,
    peeled, and chopped
1 can condensed cream of
    celery soup
1 cup milk

6 slices bacon, fried crisp
    and crumbled,
    drippings reserved
1 envelope packaged cheese
    sauce
$1/2$ bell pepper, chopped
$1/2$ onion, chopped

Preheat oven to 350 degrees.

Mix the sliced potatoes with chiles, soup, milk, bacon, and cheese sauce. Sauté the bell pepper and onion in bacon drippings until limp; add to the potato mixture.

Cover the casserole and bake $1\frac{1}{2}$ hours.

Serves 8.

Green Chile Mashed Potatoes

4 servings instant or fresh
   mashed potatoes
$1/4$ cup canned or frozen green
   chiles, chopped

$3/4$ cup Colby or longhorn
   cheese, grated
Salt and pepper to taste

    Preheat oven to 350 degrees.
    Prepare the mashed potatoes according to the instructions and add the remaining ingredients. Spread the mixture in a buttered casserole and bake 10 to 15 minutes or until the cheese has melted and blended with the potatoes.
    Serves 4.

Roundup Mashed Potatoes

1 can (4 oz.) whole green
   chiles
6 cups prepared mashed
   potatoes, fresh or
   instant

2 eggs, separated
$3/4$ cup cheddar cheese,
   shredded
$1/2$ cup small curd cottage
   cheese

    Preheat oven to 375 degrees.
    Chop the chiles. Combine the chiles with the mashed potatoes, egg yolks, and cheeses. Mix well.
    Beat the egg whites until stiff and fold them into the potato mixture. Turn into a 2-quart casserole and bake for 40 minutes or until browned and puffy.
    Serves 8.

Southwestern Spinach

2 pkgs. (10 oz. each) frozen
    chopped spinach
4 Tbs. butter or margarine
2 Tbs. flour
2 Tbs. onion, chopped
$^{1}/_{2}$ cup evaporated milk
$^{1}/_{2}$ cup spinach cooking water
$^{1}/_{2}$ tsp. black pepper

$^{3}/_{4}$ tsp. celery salt
$^{3}/_{4}$ tsp. garlic salt
1 cup sharp cheese, grated
1 tsp. Worcestershire sauce
1 can (4 oz.) green chiles,
    chopped
Buttered bread crumbs

Preheat oven to 350 degrees.

Cook the spinach according to the package directions. Drain, reserving $^{1}/_{2}$ cup liquid.

Sauté the onion in butter until soft. Blend in the flour. Add the milk and water slowly, stirring constantly to avoid lumps. Cook until smooth and thickened.

Add the remaining ingredients except the bread crumbs. Pour into a 9-inch square baking dish and top with the bread crumbs. Bake 25 minutes.

Serves 6 to 8.

Zucchini Españolas

3 Tbs. margarine
$1^{1}/_{2}$ lbs. zucchini, cubed
$^{1}/_{2}$ cup onion, minced
6 large green chiles, chopped

1 pkg. (16 oz.) frozen whole
    kernel white corn
Salt to taste
1 cup ricotta cheese

In a large saucepan melt the margarine. Add the zucchini and simmer, covered, until tender. Add the onion and cook until translucent. Add the chiles, corn, and salt and simmer 10 minutes.

Turn off the heat and add the cheese. Mix well and let stand until the cheese is melted.

Serves 8.

Summer Squash Bake

1 cup milk, scalded
1 cup bread crumbs
2 eggs, beaten
1 lb. yellow summer squash,
    cooked, drained, and
    mashed
1 cup sharp cheddar cheese,
    diced

2 Tbs. margarine
1 tsp. salt
Black pepper to taste
3 Tbs. pimentos, chopped
1 can (4 oz.) green chiles,
    chopped

Preheat oven to 350 degrees.

Grease a 1-quart casserole. Scald the milk and add the bread crumbs, eggs, cooked squash, cheese, margarine, salt, pepper, pimentos, and green chiles.

Mix well and pour into a casserole. Set the casserole in a pan of hot water and bake 40 minutes.

Serves 6.

Variation—Stir in 1 well-beaten egg and top the casserole with buttered bread crumbs before baking.

Stuffed Zucchini

2 lbs. small, whole zucchini
$^1/_4$ cup onion, chopped
1 Tbs. butter, melted
2 eggs, slightly beaten
8 oz. canned or frozen whole
    kernel corn
1 can (4 oz.) green chiles,
    chopped

$^1/_2$ cup soda cracker crumbs
$^1/_4$ cup Parmesan cheese,
    grated
$^1/_2$ tsp. salt
Dash each of garlic powder,
    pepper, and oregano

Preheat oven to 350 degrees.

Trim the ends from the zucchini; cook in boiling water 5 to 8 minutes; drain. Cut the zucchini in half lengthwise, scoop out the centers, and chop the pulp.

Cook the onion in melted butter until tender. Combine the eggs, corn, chiles, cracker crumbs, cheese, chopped zucchini, and seasonings.

Sprinkle the zucchini shells with salt and spoon in the filling. Place in a baking dish and bake for 30 minutes. Sprinkle each squash with more Parmesan cheese.

Serves 4.

Low-Calorie Delight

2 large green chiles, peeled
    and cut into strips
1 medium zucchini, sliced
1 bunch green onions, sliced
16 cherry tomatoes
$^3/_4$ cup celery, diced

$^1/_4$ cup red bell pepper or
    pimento, diced
1 cup fresh mushrooms, sliced
$^1/_4$ tsp. oregano
$^1/_8$ tsp. black pepper
$^1/_2$ tsp. salt
3 Tbs. water

Mix all the vegetables together in a saucepan. Sprinkle with the oregano, pepper, and salt. Add the water. Cook, tightly covered, for 5 minutes, turning once gently.

Reduce the heat to a slow simmer and cook 4 to 5 minutes more, turning once or twice.

Serves 4.

Zucchini Esquibel

Peanut oil
1½ lbs. zucchini, cut into
    1-inch slices (4 cups)
3 cilantro leaves (coriander)
3 fresh or canned green
    chiles
⅛ tsp. rosemary

4 cloves garlic
1 tsp. salt
1 can (6 oz.) tomato paste
1 can (16 oz.) tomatoes
½ lb. sharp cheddar cheese,
    sliced

Preheat oven to 400 degrees.

Pour the oil to a depth of ¼ inch in a skillet and heat to 450 degrees. Fry the sliced zucchini in the oil until tender and transparent on both sides. Drain on paper towels.

Grind together the cilantro, chiles, rosemary, garlic, and salt in a blender or mortar and pestle. Combine the tomato paste and tomatoes in a saucepan and add the herb mixture. Cook, stirring, 5 minutes.

Spread the cooked zucchini in the bottom of a 12×15-inch ovenproof casserole. Pour the sauce over the zucchini and top with the cheese. Cover and bake 45 minutes.

Serves 6 to 8.

Creamy Vegetable Mélange

3 Tbs. margarine
3 Tbs. flour
1 tsp. salt
Dash pepper
1¼ cups milk

2 cups zucchini, cubed
2 cups whole kernel white
    corn, drained
½ can (4 oz.) green chiles,
    chopped (or to taste)

Make a white sauce by combining the margarine, flour, seasonings, and milk over low heat. Turn the heat up to medium and cook the sauce until it thickens, stirring often.

(continued on next page)

Meanwhile, chop the zucchini into bite-sized pieces. Add the zucchini, corn, and chiles to the thickened white sauce and bring it to a boil over medium heat. Cover, reduce heat, and simmer 15 to 20 minutes until zucchini is tender.

Serves 5 to 6.

Calabacitas Zowie

2 Tbs. margarine
1 small onion, chopped
1 large zucchini or yellow
    summer squash, diced
3 fresh green chiles, chopped

1 cup whole kernel white
    corn
1 tsp. salt
$^1/_2$ cup Old English or
    Monterey Jack cheese,
        grated

Preheat oven to 350 degrees.

Melt the margarine in a heavy saucepan. Sauté the onion until tender; add the squash, green chiles, corn, and salt and toss until well-coated with margarine and onion. Transfer to a casserole and sprinkle with the grated cheese. Cover and bake for 30 minutes.

Serves 6.

Variation—Season with garlic powder and add chopped, canned, or fresh tomatoes. Mix in 6 slices bacon, fried, crisp, and crumbled.

Variation—Add $^2/_3$ cup evaporated milk and 1 cup creamed-style corn before baking. Sprinkle with grated Parmesan cheese.

Chile-Mushroom Fritters

1 cup biscuit mix
1 cup fresh mushrooms,
   chopped
2 Tbs. green onions, chopped
4 Tbs. green chile, chopped
1 tsp. salt

$^1/_4$ tsp. celery seed
1 beaten egg yolk
$^1/_4$ cup dairy sour cream
1 egg white
Cooking oil for deep-fat frying

In mixing bowl, combine biscuit mix, mushrooms, onions, chile, salt and celery seed. Mix together egg yolk and sour cream; stir into dry ingredients just until moistened. Beat egg white to stiff peaks. Gently fold beaten egg white into mushroom mixture.

In heavy saucepan or electric deep-fat fryer, heat oil to 375 degrees. Drop batter by tablespoonfuls into hot oil. Fry about 2 minutes or until golden brown, turning once. Transfer to rack to drain.

Serves 4.

Breads, Rice, and Pasta

Southwestern Corn Bread

1 cup flour
1 cup cornmeal
1/4 cup sugar
1 Tbs. baking powder
1/2 tsp. salt
1 egg

1 cup milk
1/4 cup shortening, melted
1 cup cheddar cheese, grated
2 cans (4 oz. each) green
　chiles, chopped

Preheat oven to 425 degrees.

Sift the flour; measure and sift it again with the cornmeal, sugar, baking powder, and salt. Beat the egg slightly and add the milk and shortening.

Combine the two mixtures, stirring only until moist. Spread half the grated cheese in the bottom of a greased 8-inch square baking pan. Spread the green chiles over the cheese and top with the remaining cheese.

Pour the combined batter over the chile-cheese layer. Bake for 20 minutes or until done.

Serves 4 to 6.

Sour Cream Corn Bread

1 cup yellow cornmeal
1 1/2 tsp. salt
1 Tbs. baking powder
1 cup canned creamed-style corn
1 cup sour cream or sour
　half-and-half

2/3 cup butter or margarine,
　melted
2 eggs, well beaten
1/4 lb. cheddar cheese, grated
1 can (4 oz.) green chiles,
　chopped

Preheat oven to 350 degrees.

Stir together the cornmeal, salt, and baking powder. Add the corn, sour cream, melted butter, eggs, cheese, and chiles.

Stir until well blended. Pour into a greased 9-inch square baking dish and bake for 1 hour or until done.

Serves 6 to 9.

Corny Corn Bread

2¹/₂ cups cornmeal
1 cup sifted flour
2 Tbs. sugar
1 tsp. salt
1 Tbs. baking powder
3 eggs, beaten
¹/₂ cup milk

¹/₂ cup salad oil
1 can (16¹/₂ oz.) creamed-
  style corn
1 or 2 cans (4 oz.) green
  chiles, chopped
2 cups cheese, grated
1 large onion, chopped

Preheat oven to 425 degrees.
Mix all the dry ingredients together. Add the milk and oil to the beaten eggs. Then add this mixture to the dry ingredients and mix well.
Add the corn, chiles, cheese, and onion. Mix well. Pour into 2 greased 9-inch square baking pans. Bake 30 minutes or until done.
Serves 8 to 10.

Buttermilk Corn Bread

1 cup cornmeal
1 tsp. salt
1¹/₂ Tbs. baking powder
¹/₂ cup salad oil
2 eggs, beaten

1 cup buttermilk
1¹/₂ cups creamed-style corn
1 cup cheese, grated
1 can (4 oz.) whole green
  chiles

Preheat oven to 350 degrees.
Combine all the ingredients except the cheese and chiles.
Pour half the batter into a greased 9-inch square baking dish. Place the chiles on the batter whole or cut up. Sprinkle with half the cheese. Pour the remaining batter over the chiles and cheese. Sprinkle with the remaining cheese. Bake 1 hour or until done.
Serves 6.

Noodles with Green Chile

1 pkg. (8 oz.) noodles, cooked
   and drained
1½ cups cottage cheese
1 carton (8 oz.) sour cream
1 clove garlic, crushed

1 large onion, chopped
6 large chiles, chopped
1 can (8 oz.) black olives,
   chopped
Parmesan cheese, grated
Butter

Preheat oven to 350 degrees.

Mix the noodles with all the ingredients except the Parmesan cheese and turn into a greased 1-quart casserole. Sprinkle with the Parmesan cheese and dot with butter. Bake for 30 minutes.

Serves 6.

Yum-Yum Rice Casserole

4 cups cooked rice
1 carton (8 oz.) sour cream
1 cup cheddar or Monterey
   Jack cheese, grated

1 can condensed cream of
   celery soup
½ cup sautéed or canned
   mushrooms, chopped
1 cup green chile, chopped

Preheat oven to 375 degrees.

Mix the cooked rice with the undiluted soup, sour cream, and mushrooms. Layer a third of this mixture on the bottom of a greased 1-quart casserole. Add a layer of green chiles. Repeat this layering process twice. Top with the grated cheese and bake for 20 minutes.

Serves 6.

Hominy Grits Casserole

3 cups boiling water
3/4 cup white hominy grits
1/2 cup butter or margarine
2 cups sharp cheese, grated
1 tsp. savory salt
1/2 tsp. Worcestershire sauce

1 tsp. salt
1/8 tsp. garlic powder
2 eggs, beaten
1 can (4 oz.) green chiles,
    chopped (or more to
    taste)

Preheat oven to 350 degrees.

Cook the hominy grits in boiling water 15 minutes. Add the butter and cheese and stir until melted. Add the seasonings; then fold in the eggs and green chiles. Pour into a greased 9×12-inch casserole and bake 1 hour.

Serves 8.

Green Chile Gnocci

4 cups milk
1 1/2 tsp. salt
1 cup hominy grits, uncooked
1/2 cup margarine, cut up

1/2 to 1 cup green chiles,
    chopped
2 cups cheddar cheese,
    grated
2 eggs, lightly beaten

Combine the first 4 ingredients and cook over low heat, stirring, until the margarine is melted.

Add the remaining ingredients and pour into a greased 2-quart casserole.

Let stand at room temperature until ready to bake. Bake at 350 degrees for 1 hour. Cover the last 10 minutes. Excellent for buffets.

Serves 8.

💈 💈 💈

Green Chile Fritters

1 cup flour
1/2 tsp. salt
1 Tbs. masa or cornmeal
1 egg, slightly beaten
1 cup milk

1 Tbs. shortening
8 strips of 1 inch-wide green
*   chiles*
Hot oil

Mix the flour, salt, and masa into a bowl. Add the beaten egg, milk, and shortening. Drop the chiles into the batter. Then deep fry them in hot oil. Serve with refried beans.

Serves 4.

Traditional Favorites

Sweet Chile Albóndigas

1 egg
1/4 cup milk
2 lbs. beef or pork, boiled and
    shredded
1 1/2 cups brown sugar
1 cup raisins, chopped

1 1/2 tsp. allspice
1 tsp. salt
1 cup green chiles, chopped
1 cup flour
Cooking oil

In a small bowl beat the egg with the milk.

In a separate bowl, combine the meat, brown sugar, raisins, allspice, salt, and chiles; stir in 2 tablespoons of the egg-milk mixture.

With hands lightly coated with flour, shape the meat mixture into ovals the size of small eggs. Dip the ovals into flour and then in the remaining egg batter.

In hot oil (420 degrees) fry the ovals until golden. Drain on absorbent towels. Serve with Caramel Syrup.

Makes 24.

Variation—Dip the ovals into a batter of 4 eggs, 1 tsp. salt, and 1 tsp. flour, stiffly beaten, before frying.

Variation—Add 1/2 cup roasted piñon nuts to the meat mixture. Add 1 tsp. ground cinnamon and 1 tsp. ground nutmeg for a spicier taste.

CARMEL SYRUP:

3/4 cup sugar
2 cups water

1 tsp. vanilla extract
1 tsp. cinnamon

In a saucepan heat the sugar slowly until brown; add the remaining ingredients and bring to a boil. Serve hot over Sweet Chile Albóndigas.

In New Mexico this is a traditional holiday dish among the Spanish-surnamed population, and it is usually served at Spanish wedding feasts.

New Mexican Posole

1 3-lb. pork loin
1 pkg. (2 lbs.) frozen posole
1 large onion, diced
2 tsp. oregano
1¹/₂ tsp. garlic powder

¹/₂ tsp. thyme
2 Tbs. salt
1 tsp. black pepper
4 cans (4 oz. each) green
   chiles, chopped
   (or to taste)

Boil the pork loin until tender. Cool and cut it into 1-inch cubes.

Rinse the posole well with cool water. Place it in a large stewpot and cover it with 2 quarts of water. Simmer at least 1 hour or until the posole kernels burst.

Add the pork cubes, onions, and seasonings and simmer, covered, 6 to 8 hours, adding water if necessary. During the last hour of cooking add the green chiles.

The flavor is enhanced by cooking it a day early, refrigerating it overnight, and reheating before serving. Freezes well.

Serves 8 to 10.

Variation—Add 1 can (16 oz.) stewed tomatoes before cooking.

Variation—Substitute 2 cans (32 oz. each) white hominy, drained, for the frozen posole. Reduce the cooking time to 3 hours.

Variation—Add 2 cups of tomato juice to the posole liquid 1 hour before serving. Stir in red chile purée to taste.

Taco Tempters

1 lb. ground beef
2 medium potatoes, cooked
  and diced
$1/2$ tsp. oregano
$1/4$ tsp. garlic salt
$1/4$ tsp. salt
12 taco shells

1 small onion, chopped
$1/4$ cup green chiles, chopped
  (or more to taste)
1 cup longhorn cheese, grated
1 cup taco sauce
1 cup lettuce, shredded

Preheat oven to 250 degrees.

Sauté the ground beef in a skillet; drain off the excess fat. Add the potatoes and seasonings; mix well.

Fill each taco shell with 2 tablespoons of meat mixture, $1/2$ teaspoon onion, and 1 teaspoon green chiles. Sprinkle each taco with grated cheese. Place the tacos in a baking dish and heat until the cheese is melted.

At serving time top with taco sauce and shredded lettuce.

Makes 12 tacos.

Variation—At serving time top each taco with a dollop of guacamole.

Variation—Omit seasonings and mix sautéed ground beef with 2 cans (15 oz. each) hot chiles with beans.

Sour Cream Enchiladas

1 lb. lean ground beef
1 pkg. enchilada sauce mix
1 can (8 oz.) tomato sauce
$1^1/2$ cups boiling water
8 oz. cheddar cheese, grated
2 cups sour cream

12 corn tortillas
1 cup lettuce, chopped
1 medium tomato, chopped
1 can (4 oz.) green chiles,
  chopped

Preheat oven to 350 degrees.

Sauté the ground beef in a skillet until done; drain off the fat. In a small saucepan combine the enchilada sauce mix, tomato sauce, and water; simmer 10 minutes. Add $1/2$ cup of this mixture to the meat along with half of the grated cheese.

Lightly fry each tortilla and drain on paper towels. Place 2 table-spoons of the meat mixture on each tortilla and top each with 1 tablespoon of the sour cream. Roll each tortilla and place seam side down in a greased casserole.

Spread the remaining sour cream over the top and sprinkle with the green chiles and remaining cheese. Finally, spoon the enchilada sauce mixture over all.

Bake for 20 to 30 minutes or until the enchiladas are well heated and the cheese is melted. Top with lettuce and tomatoes before serving.

Serves 6 to 8.

Mrs. Lujan's Green Chile Stew

1 pt. green chiles, peeled
   and chopped
Onion and garlic salt to taste

1^1/$_2$ lbs. beef or pork, cubed, or
   lean ground beef,
1 medium onion, chopped
Salt and pepper to taste

Season the chopped chiles with onion and garlic salt.

Sauté the meat with the onion until brown. Drain. Season with salt and pepper to taste.

Add the chiles and hot water to the desired amount and simmer until the meat is tender.

Using this recipe as a basic stew, you can add uncooked cubed potatoes, tomatoes, or even chopped cabbage. It can also be added to a pot of beans or poured over a macaroni and cheese casserole.

Serves 6.

Sour Cream Enchiladas in a Stack

2 cans chicken consommé
1 cup water or milk
2 Tbs. flour
1 cup cooked chicken
$^1/_2$ to 1 cup green chiles, chopped
Salt to taste
1 clove garlic, mashed
12 corn tortillas

1$^1/_2$ cups Monterey Jack or cheddar cheese, grated
1 medium onion, chopped
2 cups sour cream
4 eggs, lightly fried or poached (optional)
Lettuce, coarsely chopped
2 tomatoes, cut into eighths

Combine the consommé with the water or milk; add the flour and blend well. Cook until thickened, adding more flour mixed with water if desired.

Add the chicken and green chiles and season with salt and garlic. Lightly fry the tortillas if desired. Combine 1 cup of the grated cheese, onion, and sour cream.

Assemble the enchiladas by placing a spoonful of sauce on each warm plate followed by a tortilla, sauce, and a spoonful of the sour cream mixture. Continue until each of 4 plates has 3 tortillas and all the sauce is used.

Place the plates in a hot oven to melt the cheese; place an egg on top of each and sprinkle with the remaining cheese. Warm in the oven briefly. Top and encircle each enchilada with chopped lettuce and garnish with tomatoes.

Serves 4.

Burritos with Chile-Cheese Sauce

BURRITOS:

1 lb. ground beef
1/2 cup onions, chopped
1/4 tsp. cumin
1/2 tsp. oregano
1 tsp. garlic salt
1 Tbs. cooking oil

1 can (15 oz.) pinto beans,
    drained
1/2 cup cheddar cheese, grated
Salt to taste
6 white flour tortillas
4 oz. canned or frozen green
    chiles, chopped

Preheat oven to 350 degrees.

Brown the ground beef in a 10-inch skillet; drain off the fat. Add the onions and sauté until translucent. Add the spices.

Heat the oil in a small skillet and add the pinto beans. Mash the beans with a potato masher and sprinkle them with half the cheddar cheese. Cook over low heat until the cheese is melted; add salt to taste.

Divide the bean mixture evenly among 6 tortillas; top each with evenly divided meat mixture. Spoon green chiles over the meat and top with the remaining cheddar cheese. Roll up each tortilla and place it, seam side down, on a greased cookie sheet. Top with Chile-Cheese Sauce.

CHILE-CHEESE SAUCE:

1 can condensed cheddar
    cheese soup

1 can (4 oz.) green chiles,
    chopped

Heat the soup in a small saucepan over medium heat; add the chopped chiles and mix well. Pour over rolled burritos and heat 15 to 20 minutes.

Serves 3 to 6.

Chile with Fresh Corn

2 lbs. beef, pork, or mutton,
　cubed
3 Tbs. cooking oil
Fresh corn scraped from
　3 cobs
10 to 12 green chiles, chopped

2 medium tomatoes, chopped
$^{1}/_{4}$ cup onion, chopped
1 clove garlic, minced
1 tsp. salt (or to taste)

　　Put the meat in a large cooking pot with the oil and sauté it until browned; add the corn, chiles, tomatoes, onion, garlic, and salt with enough water to cover.

　　Cover the pan and simmer for 1 hour.

　　Serves 6 to 8.

Main Dishes
with Meat

Stuffed Cabbage, Spanish Style

1 medium head cabbage
Boiling water
1 lb. lean ground beef
$^1/_2$ lb. pork sausage
1 small onion, peeled and
 grated
1$^1/_2$ cups green chiles, chopped
$^1/_2$ tsp. garlic salt (optional)

Salt to taste
1 medium onion, chopped
1$^1/_2$ cups apples, peeled and
 thinly sliced
1 can (16 oz.) sauerkraut,
 rinsed and drained
1 cup chicken broth
1 cup tomato juice

Cut out and discard the core of the cabbage and put the remaining cabbage in a saucepan. Cover it with boiling water and simmer for 5 minutes. Remove the cabbage from the water and cool. Pull the leaves off one at a time until you have 10 large leaves.

Combine the ground beef and sausage and cook 15 to 20 minutes. Add the chopped onion and cook until the onion is translucent. Drain off the excess fat. Add the green chiles, garlic salt, and salt and mix well. Cool.

Preheat oven to 350 degrees. Then place $^1/_3$ cup of the meat and chile mixture in each cabbage leaf, roll up, and secure with toothpicks.

Mix the chopped onion, apples, and sauerkraut. Spread half of this mixture on the bottom of a large baking dish. Place the cabbage rolls on the sauerkraut. Spread the remaining sauerkraut on top.

Mix chicken broth and tomato juice and pour over the rolls. Cover and bake for 1 hour.

Serves 5.

Stuffed Green Chiles

12 to 14 green chiles
3/4 cup rice
2 lbs. ground chuck
1/2 cup onion, chopped
1 egg
1 clove garlic, minced
2 tsp. parsley flakes or 1 Tbs.
   fresh parsley, chopped

Salt and pepper to taste
1/4 cup margarine
1/3 cup flour
2 cans (8 oz. each) tomato
   sauce
6 cups water

Preheat oven to 350 degrees.

Peel the green chiles, remove stems and seeds, and slit them down the sides.

Combine the rice, meat, onion, egg, garlic, parsley, salt, and pepper. Stuff the chiles with the mixture.

Melt the margarine and add the flour. Cook until the flour is lightly browned and remove from heat. Add the tomato sauce and 3 cups water.

Add the stuffed chiles and the remaining water; the water should just cover the chiles.

Bring to a boil; then place in oven and bake for 3 hours.

Serves 5 to 6.

Tampico Stuffed Chiles

1 lb. ground beef
1 medium onion, chopped
1 can (4 oz.) green chiles,
    chopped
1/2 lb. processed American
    cheese
1/4 cup milk

1/2 tsp. salt
20 green chiles, roasted and
    peeled
20 strips cheddar cheese
1/2 cup pitted ripe olives,
    sliced

Preheat oven to 350 degrees.

Brown the ground beef and onion in a skillet; drain off the fat. Add the chopped green chiles, processed cheese, milk, and salt.

Spread the whole chiles open and arrange them in the bottom of a baking pan. Fill the chiles with the meat sauce; top each with a strip of cheddar cheese, and sprinkle each with sliced olives.

Bake, uncovered, for 7 to 10 minutes or until the cheese is slightly melted.

Serves 6.

Sanchez Tam O'Shanter

1 pkg. (10 oz.) frozen leaf
    spinach
1 1/4 lbs. lean ground beef
1/2 medium onion, chopped
Salt to taste

1 can (4 oz.) green chiles,
    chopped
6 eggs, beaten
Garlic salt to taste (optional)
Tomatoes, cut into wedges
    (optional)

Cook the spinach according to the directions on the package; drain thoroughly. In a large, non-stick skillet, sauté the meat, onion, and salt; drain off the excess fat. Add the spinach and chiles and mix well. Gently pour the beaten eggs over the meat mixture. Cook over medium heat until the eggs are set.

Garnish with tomato wedges if desired.

Serves 3 to 4.

Great Green Bean Chile

2 lbs. ground beef
1 small onion, chopped
3 packages (10 oz. each) French-style
   frozen green beans, undrained
1 can (16 oz.) whole tomatoes,
   undrained

1 can (8 oz.) tomato sauce
1 can (4 oz.) green chiles,
   chopped
$1^1/_2$ tsp. salt

Brown the ground beef with the onion in a skillet.

In a separate large pan combine the green beans (thawed), tomatoes, tomato sauce, and green chiles; simmer $^1/_2$ hour, stirring occasionally.

When the meat and onions are done, add to the green bean mixture and simmer slowly 20 minutes. Add salt and mix well.

Delicious served with flour tortillas or corn chips and dip.

Serves 8.

Little Boats

3 medium eggplants
2 Tbs. olive oil
1 medium onion, chopped
1 clove garlic, minced
2 stalks celery, chopped
1/2 green pepper, chopped
1 lb. ground lamb or beef
1 can (16 oz.) whole tomatoes,
   drained and chopped
1 can (8 oz.) tomato sauce

1/3 cup tomato liquid
6 to 8 green chiles, chopped
3/4 cup quick cooking rice
2 Tbs. parsley flakes
1/2 tsp. dried mint, crumbled
1/2 tsp. dill weed
1 1/2 tsp. salt
3/4 tsp. freshly ground black
   pepper
1/4 cup sesame seeds

Preheat oven to 350 degrees.

Slice the eggplants in half lengthwise. Scoop out the pulp, leaving 1-inch-thick shells; reserve the pulp and shells.

Heat the oil. Sauté the onion and garlic 2 minutes. Add the celery and green pepper and sauté 2 minutes more. Add the lamb and cook until the meat is browned. Drain off the fat.

Chop the eggplant pulp and add to the meat mixture. Cook, stirring occasionally, 10 minutes. Add the tomatoes, tomato sauce, tomato liquid, and green chiles and cook 5 minutes more.

Remove the mixture from the heat and add the rice, parsley, mint, dill weed, salt, and pepper. Mix well.

Salt and pepper the eggplant shells and fill them with the meat mixture.

Toast the sesame seeds by placing them in a small pan over moderate heat just until browned, stirring occasionally. Sprinkle the seeds over the tops of the filled eggplants.

Arrange the eggplants in a buttered baking dish and add 1/4 inch boiling water. Cover and bake for 1 hour or until the eggplants are tender.

Serves 6.

Big Wheel Chile Burger

1 Tbs. instant minced onion
1/2 cup milk
1 1/2 lbs. ground beef
1 egg, slightly beaten
1/2 cup quick-cooking rolled
   oats
2 tsp. salt
1/4 tsp. coarsely ground black
   pepper

1/4 tsp. bottled browning sauce
1 can (8 oz.) spaghetti sauce
   with mushrooms
1 can (4 oz.) green chiles,
   chopped
1 can (8 oz.) pinto beans with
   liquid

Soak the onion in milk 5 minutes; mix in the ground beef, egg, oats, salt, and pepper. Mound in a 10-inch skillet. With a wooden spoon handle, score in 5 or 6 wedges; brush the top lightly with bottled browning sauce.

Combine the spaghetti sauce, chiles, and pinto beans. Pour over the meat mixture. Simmer, uncovered, 20 to 25 minutes or until done.

Serve the wedges of burger on crusty French bread slices; spoon the sauce over.

Serves 5 or 6.

Green Chile Goulash

1 cup green chiles, chopped
1 cup onions, chopped
3 Tbs. cooking oil
1 lb. ground beef

4 cups whole grain corn
2 cans (8 oz. each) tomato
  sauce
1 tsp. salt

Brown the chiles and onions in oil. Add the ground beef and stir until browned. Drain. Add the remaining ingredients and simmer slowly for 20 minutes.
Serves 4.

Variation—Use 1 16-oz. can peeled tomatoes instead of the sauce and add $1/4$ tsp. cumin and $1/2$ cup chopped celery. Stir in 1 cup cooked macaroni and lay strips of American cheese over the mixture. Heat until it melts.

Variation—Add $1/2$ tsp. crushed oregano and $1/4$ tsp. garlic powder. Serve over rice or macaroni.

Crusted Green Chile Loaf

1 pkg. (8 oz.) uncooked
  crescent rolls
1 egg
1 lb. ground beef

$1/2$ tsp. salt
$1/4$ cup onion, chopped
$1/3$ cup instant oatmeal
$1 1/2$ cups green chiles, chopped

Preheat oven to 400 degrees.
Flatten the crescent roll dough into a 9×10-inch rectangle. Place it on a cookie sheet and bake for 3 to 5 minutes.
Combine the next 5 ingredients. Spread the mixture over the partially baked crescent dough. Spread green chiles over the meat.
Roll the mixture to fit a $9 \times 5 \times 2 1/2$-inch loaf pan. Place in the loaf pan and bake for 10 minutes; then reduce oven temperature to 350 degrees and continue baking for 20 to 30 minutes. Top with your favorite cheese sauce.
Serves 6.

Zesty Meat Loaf

$1/2$ cup onion, finely chopped
1 lb. ground beef
2 eggs, beaten
1 cup mashed potatoes
$1/2$ tsp. paprika
1 tsp. ground coriander
2 Tbs. Parmesan cheese, grated
$1/4$ tsp. black pepper

1 cup evaporated milk
1 cup water
1 cup green chiles, chopped
$1/2$ cup sharp cheddar cheese,
   grated
10 Wheat Thins, mashed
$1/2$ tsp. garlic salt

Parboil the onion 20 minutes in enough water to cover. Add the onion and liquid to the meat and mix in remaining ingredients. Place the mixture in a greased loaf pan and bake, covered at 350 degrees, for 1 hour. Uncover the last 10 minutes to brown the meat loaf.

Serves 6.

Chile Stew Enchiladas

$1^1/2$ lbs. ground beef
10 large green chiles,
   peeled and chopped
1 clove garlic, chopped
Water or broth

12 corn tortillas
1 large onion, chopped
12 slices processed cheese,
   shredded

Preheat oven to 350 degrees.

Brown the ground beef; drain and add the chopped chiles and garlic and enough water or broth to make a stew-like consistency. Bring the mixture to a boil and simmer for 15 minutes.

Lightly fry the tortillas until soft. Place a small amount of chopped onions and shredded cheese in each tortilla and roll. Place in a 9×13-inch casserole.

Pour the chile stew over the enchiladas. Sprinkle with additional cheese and onions. Cover and heat in the oven until the cheese melts, about 8 minutes.

Serves 4 to 6.

Cottage Enchiladas

1 1/2 lbs. lean ground beef
1/2 cup onions, chopped
Salt to taste
1 pkg. (12) corn tortillas
1 1/2 lbs. longhorn cheese,
   grated

1 cup sour cream
1 cup cottage cheese
2 cans (8 oz. ea.) taco sauce
1/2 cup green chiles, chopped

Preheat oven to 350 degrees.

Sauté the ground beef until done; drain off the fat and season with salt to taste; add the onions and cook until they are translucent.

Lightly fry the tortillas and drain on paper towels. Onto each tortilla place 1 tablespoon each of the meat, grated cheese, sour cream, and cottage cheese; roll the tortillas and place them in a 12×7-inch baking dish with the seam sides down.

Mix the taco sauce and green chiles and pour over the rolled tortillas. Sprinkle with the remaining grated cheese and bake for 40 minutes.

Serves 6.

Mediterranean Lasagne

1½ lbs. ground beef
½ lb. Italian sausage, sliced
3 Tbs. olive oil
1 to 2 cloves garlic, minced
1 medium onion, chopped
Salt and pepper to taste
3 cans (8 oz. each) spaghetti
   sauce
2 Tbs. spaghetti sauce
   seasoning
½ can (6 oz.) tomato paste

6 Tbs. Parmesan cheese,
   grated
2 cups cottage cheese
1 Tbs. parsley, finely
   chopped
2 eggs
1 pkg. (16 oz.) lasagne
2 cups green chiles,
   chopped
½ lb. mozzarella cheese,
   thinly sliced

Brown the ground beef and sausage in oil. Add the garlic and onion; season with salt and pepper to taste. Drain off the fat.

Combine the spaghetti sauce, spaghetti sauce seasoning, and tomato paste and simmer 30 minutes. Add 4 tablespoons of Parmesan cheese.

Combine the cottage cheese, parsley, and eggs and mix together with a spoon.

Cook the lasagne according to package directions. Drain.

Lightly grease a 13×9-inch baking pan. Spread 1 cup of sauce on the bottom. Top with strips of lasagne; spread with part of the cheese filling; add another layer of lasagne; spread with part of the meat filling, then with 1 cup of green chiles.

Repeat the layers, ending with the sauce and last cup of green chiles. Top with the sliced mozzarella cheese, sprinkle with more Parmesan cheese, and add more sauce if desired.

Bake at 350 degrees for 30 minutes. Let stand 5 to 10 minutes before cutting the lasagne in squares.

Serves 10.

Southwestern Lasagne

1 can (16 oz.) tomatoes
1 can (10 oz.) red enchilada
   sauce
$1/4$ cup pitted ripe olives,
   sliced
$1/2$ cup green chiles, chopped
1 tsp. salt

2 cups Basic Ground Beef
   Mixture
$1/2$ cup oil
8 corn tortillas
4 oz. longhorn cheese,
   shredded

In a medium saucepan combine the tomatoes, enchilada sauce, olives, chiles, and salt. Add the meat mixture and simmer, covered, for 20 minutes, stirring occasionally.

Heat the oil in a skillet. Cut 2 tortillas into quarters and cook all the tortillas in oil until crisp and brown. Drain. Set the quartered tortillas aside and break up the remaining 6.

Spread a third of the meat mixture in a 9-inch square baking dish. Top with half the cheese, then half the broken tortillas. Repeat the layers, ending with the meat mixture.

Top with the quartered tortillas and bake at 350 degrees for 30 minutes. If desired, sprinkle $1/2$ cup shredded cheese over the top and heat until the cheese melts.

Let stand 5 minutes before serving.

Serves 4 to 5.

BASIC GROUND BEEF MIXTURE:

1 lb. ground beef
$1/2$ cup celery, chopped

$1/2$ cup onion, chopped
$1/4$ cup green pepper,
      chopped

Combine all the ingredients in a large skillet and cook, stirring, over medium heat until the meat is browned and the vegetables are tender. Drain. Cool quickly.

Great Green Chile Casserole

12 corn tortillas
1 can (16 oz.) hominy,
  drained
2 cups cheese, grated
1 onion, chopped

2 cans (4 oz. each) green
  chiles, chopped
1 lb. ground beef, browned
1 can (16 oz.) green chile
  salsa or taco or
  enchilada sauce

Preheat oven to 350 degrees.

Quickly fry the tortillas in hot oil. Cover the bottom of a 9×13-inch casserole with half the tortillas. Layer all of the hominy, 1 cup cheese, half the onion, and half the chopped green chiles over half the tortillas.

Cover with the remaining tortillas, the ground beef, the remaining cheese, onion, and green chiles. Pour the salsa over the top and sprinkle with additional grated cheese.

Bake for 30 minutes. Freezes well.

Serves 8 to 10.

Upside-Down Casserole

1 lb. lean ground beef
1 Tbs. cooking oil
2 Tbs. onion, chopped
1 1/2 cups water
1 tsp. salt
4 or 5 green chiles, chopped
1 cup yellow cornmeal
1 cup sifted all-purpose flour

1/4 cup sugar
4 tsp. baking powder
1/2 tsp. salt
1/2 cup milk
1 egg
1/4 cup shortening
3/4 cup cheddar cheese, grated

Preheat oven to 425 degrees.

In a skillet brown the ground beef in a small amount of oil; add the chopped onion and sauté until the meat is browned. Add the water, 1 tsp. salt, and chopped chiles; simmer for 5 minutes.

In a medium bowl sift together the cornmeal, flour, sugar, baking powder, and 1/2 tsp.salt. Add the remaining ingredients except the cheese and beat until smooth, about 1 minute.

Grease a 9×9-inch square baking pan. Pour the meat mixture into the pan; sprinkle on the grated cheese. Spread the cornmeal mixture over the meat and bake for 20 to 25 minutes. When the casserole is done, let it sit in the pan at room temperature for 10 minutes. Then invert the casserole onto a platter (like an upside-down cake). Cut it into squares and serve immediately.

Serves 9.

Sunday Salon Casserole

3 lbs. ground beef
1 large onion, chopped
Salt and pepper to taste
3 cans (15 oz. each) pinto beans
3 cans (16 oz. each) stewed tomatoes

3 cans (4 oz. each) green chiles, chopped
1 doz. tortillas, cut into bite-size pieces
1 1/2 lbs. cheddar cheese, grated
2 cans (15 oz. each) enchilada sauce (hot or mild)

Preheat oven to 325 degrees.

Fry the meat and onion until the meat is brown; drain off the fat. Season the mixture to taste with salt and pepper. Add the pinto beans, stewed tomatoes, and chiles; simmer for 15 minutes.

Pour the mixture into a large casserole; stir in the tortilla bits, and top with the cheese. Pour the enchilada sauce over top and bake for 1 to 1½ hours, stirring occasionally.

Serves 30.

🌶 🌶 🌶

Hearty Casserole

1 lb. lean ground beef	1 can (16 oz.) tomatoes,
1 lb. potatoes, grated	cut up
1 small onion, chopped	2 cups water
1 clove garlic, minced	1 medium bag (9 oz.) corn
1 tsp. salt	chips
1 cup green chiles, chopped	8 oz. longhorn cheese,
	grated

Preheat oven to 325 degrees.

Sauté the ground beef slowly in a deep-frying pan. Drain off the fat and add the potatoes, onion, garlic, salt, chiles, and tomatoes together with 2 cups of water. Cover and simmer for 30 minutes.

In the bottom of a shallow casserole, layer half the bag of corn chips and half of the grated cheese. Then spread with the meat mixture and top with the remaining cheese and corn chips. Bake for 30 minutes.

Serves 8.

Weekday Casserole

2 cups pork or beef, cubed
3 Tbs. margarine
3 medium zucchini squash,
  sliced
1 large onion, thinly sliced
1/2 cup water

1 pkg. (16 oz.) frozen whole
  kernel white corn
1 can (16 oz.) whole tomatoes
5 large green chiles, chopped
1/4 tsp. garlic salt
Salt to taste

Preheat oven to 350 degrees.

Brown the cubed meat in 1 tablespoon margarine; add the zucchini, onion, remaining margarine, and 1/2 cup water. Bring to a boil and simmer 10 minutes.

Add the remaining ingredients and pour into a buttered casserole. Bake 20 minutes.

Serves 4 to 6.

Macaroni-Green Chile Pie

1 lb. ground beef
1/2 cup onion, chopped
1 clove garlic, finely minced
2 Tbs. oil
1 cup tomatoes
4 Tbs. tomato paste
1 tsp. sugar
1/4 tsp. oregano
1/4 tsp. dill seed

Salt and pepper to taste
6 oz. elbow macaroni
5 Tbs. Parmesan cheese,
   grated
2 eggs, slightly beaten
1/2 cup cheddar cheese, grated
1/2 cup cottage cheese
1/2 cup green chiles, chopped

Brown the ground beef with the onion and garlic in oil; drain off the excess fat. Add the tomatoes, tomato paste, sugar, and seasonings and simmer 30 minutes.

Preheat oven to 375 degrees. Cook the macaroni according to the package directions; drain.

Combine the macaroni, Parmesan cheese, and eggs. Place in a 10-inch pie pan and spread as for a crust. Bake 15 minutes.

Spread the meat mixture over the baked "crust." Combine the cottage cheese with the green chiles and spread over the meat mixture. Cover loosely with foil and bake 15 minutes more.

Remove the foil, sprinkle with the cheddar cheese, and return to the oven for 5 more minutes.

Serves 6.

Anglo-Style "Carnitas"

1 lb. sirloin steak or other
   tender cut of beef
1 cup bottled Italian salad
   dressing
1 medium onion, thinly sliced
$1/4$ tsp. salt
2 tsp. green chiles,
   chopped

6 flour tortillas
2 Tbs. margarine
1 carton (8 oz.) sour
   cream
$1/2$ cup green chiles,
   chopped

Dice the meat into $1/2$-inch cubes. Marinate the meat with the dressing, onion slices, salt, and 2 teaspoons green chiles for at least 24 hours.

Preheat oven to 350 degrees. Butter one side of each tortilla. Toast each tortilla lightly, but not crisp, then set aside.

Place the meat mixture in a skillet and cook for 20 minutes. Drain. Mix the sour cream and $1/2$ cup chopped chiles. Mound the meat on the tortillas, distributing evenly. Place a dab of sour cream mixture on top. Fold or roll.

Place in a greased baking pan, cover, and bake for 30 minutes. Serves 6.

Steak Mexican Style

3 lbs. round steak
   (serving size pieces)
$1/4$ cup lard
$1^1/2$ tsp. flour
2 carrots, diced
2 green chiles, chopped

2 onions, diced
1 can pimentos, chopped
2 cups tomatoes, chopped
$1/2$ cup fresh peas
Salt and pepper to taste

Rub meat with salt and pepper. Pound all the flour possible into meat and brown in hot lard. Add remaining ingredients, cover, and simmer on low heat about $2^1/2$ hours.

Serves 6.

Green Chile Stroganoff

1/4 cup butter or margarine
1 medium onion, chopped
1 can (4 oz.) mushrooms,
 sliced
Garlic to taste
2 lbs. lean beef, cubed
 and rolled in flour

2 cups water
2 beef bouillon cubes
1 can (4 oz.) green chiles,
 chopped
1 cup sour cream
1 pkg. (8 oz.) noodles

Sauté the onion and mushrooms in butter with the garlic. Brown the cubed beef in this mixture. Drain off the excess fat.

Add the water and bouillon cubes. Cover and simmer 2 hours. Add the green chiles and simmer 10 more minutes. Remove from the heat and stir in the sour cream.

Cook the noodles according to the package directions. Serve the Stroganoff over the noodles.

Serves 4.

Puerto de Luna Green Chile Special

6 steaks, cubed
2 Tbs. cooking oil
3 Tbs. flour
3 cups milk

6 green chiles, chopped
1/4 tsp. garlic powder
Salt to taste

Brown the cubed steaks on both sides and set aside. Combine the oil and flour in a saucepan and brown well. Add the milk and chopped green chiles, stirring constantly until thickened.

Add the garlic powder and salt to taste and stir. Place the cubed steaks in a casserole and pour the gravy over. Warm in the oven.

Serves 6.

Round Steak Roll Ups

1½ lbs. round steak, cut
  ¼ inch thick
Salt and pepper
3 green chiles, peeled and
  halved
1 can condensed onion
  soup
1 clove garlic, minced
2 cups fresh bread crumbs

3 Tbs. parsley, chopped
2 hard-cooked eggs, chopped
¼ cup Parmesan cheese,
  grated
¼ cup butter
½ cup fresh mushrooms,
  chopped
1 cup dry red wine

Pound the steak until very thin; then cut it into 6 long pieces. Sprinkle with salt and pepper.

Place the halved chiles over the strips of meat.

Sauté the garlic in ¼ cup butter until golden. Add the crumbs and sauté briefly until just golden. Stir in the parsley, hard-cooked eggs, and Parmesan cheese.

Spoon some of this mixture on each piece of meat. Roll up and fasten with toothpicks.

Brown the rolled meat on all sides in ¼ cup butter. Add the onion soup, mushrooms, and wine. Cover and simmer 1 hour or until the meat is tender. Thicken pan juices if desired and serve with noodles.

Serves 6.

Chicken Mexicana

1 broiler-fryer chicken, cut up
½ cup butter or margarine
1 tsp. salt
½ tsp. paprika
Dash pepper
1 pkg. (6 oz.) tortilla chips
1 can (4 oz.) enchilada
  sauce

1 can (4 oz.) green chiles,
  chopped
1 cup cheddar cheese,
  shredded
½ cup green onion, chopped
1 can (2½ oz.) pitted black
  olives, sliced

Preheat oven to 375 degrees.

Wash the chicken and pat dry. Arrange it in a single layer, skin side up, in a large shallow baking pan.

Melt the butter and pour it over chicken; sprinkle with salt, paprika, and pepper. Bake, uncovered, for 60 minutes.

Crumble the tortilla chips coarsely and sprinkle over the chicken. Add the enchilada sauce and chopped chiles. Sprinkle with the cheese, then the onion and olives. Return to the oven for 15 minutes or until the cheese is melted.

Serves 6.

🌶 🌶 🌶

Chicken with Pumpkin Seed Sauce

1 3-lb. chicken, cut into
  serving pieces
Salt and freshly ground black
  pepper
2 Tbs. oil
1/2 cup pumpkin seeds
  (pipians or pepitas)

1/4 cup blanched almonds
1/4 tsp. cumin seeds
1 clove garlic, finely chopped
1 can (4 oz.) green chiles,
  seeded and chopped
1/4 cup parsley, chopped
1 cup chicken broth

Season the chicken pieces with salt and pepper and brown them on all sides in the oil. Pour off the extra oil.

Toast the pumpkin seeds, almonds, and cumin seeds in a hot, dry skillet over low heat, shaking often, until the almonds are golden.

Grind the toasted mixture in a blender; add the garlic, chiles, and parsley and mix well. Gradually stir in the broth. Pour into a saucepan. Bring to a boil and pour over the chicken. Cover and simmer 40 minutes, or until the chicken is done.

Serves 4.

Chicken Breasts Sauterne with Chile and Avocado

4 large chicken breasts, split
   and skinned
1 1/2 tsp. salt
1 tsp. paprika
1/4 cup flour
1/4 cup shortening or salad oil
1/4 cup onion, finely chopped
1/3 cup catsup
3 Tbs. white wine vinegar

1 tsp. Worcestershire sauce
3/4 cup sauterne or other dry
   white wine
4 cups rice, cooked
1 can (4 oz.) green chiles,
   chopped
1 large avocado, peeled and
   sliced

Dust the chicken with a mixture of salt, paprika, and flour. Brown the chicken in shortening or oil.

Combine the onion, catsup, vinegar, Worcestershire sauce, and wine and pour over the chicken. Cover and simmer about 45 minutes or until the chicken is tender.

Mound the hot rice in the center of a hot platter and arrange the chicken breasts around it. Stir the chiles into the sauce and spoon it over the chicken. Arrange the avocado slices between the chicken breasts, pinwheel style.

Serves 8.

Pollo Ranchero

3 medium tomatoes, finely
   chopped
2 large green chiles, finely
   chopped
1 medium onion, finely chopped
1 cup chicken broth
$^1/_2$ tsp. salt
1 small green jalapeño
   chile, finely chopped

3 chicken breasts, boned and
   poached
2 Tbs. vegetable oil
2 Tbs. flour
3 Tbs. chile powder
2 cups water
$^1/_2$ tsp. salt
$^1/_2$ cup Monterey Jack cheese
   grated (optional)

Preheat oven to 400 degrees.

In a saucepan mix together the tomatoes, green chiles, onion, and chicken; bring the mixture to a boil. Cover and simmer $^1/_2$ hour or until the vegetables are soft. Add the salt and jalapeño chile.

While the sauce is cooking, poach the chicken breasts 10 minutes in boiling, salted water.

In another pan blend the flour, oil, and chile powder; add the water and salt and bring to a boil. Simmer gently for 5 minutes, stirring occasionally. Pour this sauce into a 9-inch square baking dish and place the chicken breasts on top.

Pour the green chiles and tomato sauce over the chicken and sprinkle generously with grated cheese; bake until the chicken is tender and cheese is thoroughly melted.

Makes 3 generous servings or 6 conservative ones.

Noodle Chicken

2 pkgs. (8 oz. each) medium
   noodles
½ cup onion, chopped
2 Tbs. butter or margarine
3 cans condensed cream of
   chicken soup

3 Tbs. green chiles, finely
   chopped
2 Tbs. pimentos, chopped
4 cups cooked chicken, cubed
Salt and pepper to taste
3 cups cheddar cheese,
   shredded

Preheat oven to 350 degrees.

Cook the noodles according to the package directions and drain.

Sauté the onion in the butter until tender. Stir in the soup, chiles, and pimentos.

In a greased 9×13-inch casserole layer half the noodles, then half the soup mixture, then half the chicken. Season. Repeat the layers. Top with cheese. Bake, uncovered, for 45 minutes.

Serves 8 to 12.

Gourmet Enchilada Parmesan

2 pkgs. (3 oz. each) cream
   cheese
2 cups heavy cream
3/4 cup onions, finely chopped
2 whole cooked chicken breasts,
   boned and shredded
6 green chiles, peeled
1 can (10 oz.) Mexican green
   tomatoes, drained
2 canned serrano chiles,
   chopped

5 tsp. fresh coriander,
   (cilantro), chopped
1/4 cup chicken broth
1 egg
1 1/2 tsp. salt
1/4 tsp. freshly ground black
   pepper
12 corn tortillas
3 Tbs. lard or oil
1/3 cup Parmesan cheese,
   grated

Preheat oven to 350 degrees.

Beat the cream cheese until smooth; then beat in 1/2 cup of the cream, 3 tablespoons at a time. Stir in the onions and chicken and mix thoroughly.

Remove the seeds from the green chiles and chop. Place the chiles in a blender with the tomatoes, canned chiles, coriander, and 1/4 cup chicken broth. Blend at high speed until the mixture is a smooth purée.

Pour in the remaining cream, egg, salt, and pepper. Blend 10 seconds longer. Transfer to a large bowl.

Dip the tortillas in the tomato mixture; then lightly fry them in hot lard or oil until limp. Place 1/4 cup of the chicken filling in the center of each tortilla and roll up.

Place the enchiladas seam side down in a shallow 8×12-inch baking dish. Pour the remaining chile-tomato mixture over the enchiladas and sprinkle the Parmesan cheese over top. Bake 15 minutes or until cheese melts and enchiladas are lightly browned.

Serves 6.

Mickey's Mousse

2 envelopes unflavored
  gelatin
2 cups chicken broth
1/3 cup green onions, chopped
1 tsp. salt
1 tsp. grated lemon rind
1 cup dry white wine
1 tsp. Worcestershire sauce
1 cup heavy cream, whipped

1 cup mayonnaise
3 Tbs. green chiles, chopped
2 cups cooked chicken,
  chopped
1 cup cooked ham, chopped
3 Tbs. fresh parsley, minced
Watercress and spiced peach
  and pear halves for
  garnish

Soften the gelatin in 1/2 cup of the broth. Heat the remaining broth to boiling, add the softened gelatin, and stir until it is dissolved.

Add the green onions, salt, and grated lemon rind; then blend in the wine and Worcestershire sauce.

Chill until the mixture thickens; then fold in the whipped cream, mayonnaise, and green chiles. Add the chicken, ham, and parsley and blend gently but thoroughly. Pour into a greased 2½-quart mold and refrigerate until firm.

Unmold on a chilled platter and surround with watercress. Garnish with spiced peach and pear halves.

Serves 6 to 8.

Chicken-Tomato Casserole

1 onion, chopped
2 Tbs. butter or margarine
1 or 2 cans (4 oz.) green
    chiles, chopped
2 cups tomato juice or 1 can
    (16 oz.) stewed tomatoes
1 tsp. cumin
1 clove garlic

1 tsp. celery seed
2 cups half-and-half or
    2 cups chicken broth
Salt and pepper to taste
3 cups cooked chicken,
    cubed
12 corn tortillas
2 cups cheese, grated

Preheat oven to 350 degrees.

Sauté the onion in butter. Add the chiles, tomato juice or tomatoes, cumin, crushed garlic, celery seed, salt, and pepper. Add the cream or broth and chicken.

Lightly fry the tortillas or dip them in sauce and layer them in a 9×13-inch casserole with the chicken and sauce. Pour any leftover sauce over the casserole. Sprinkle with cheese. Bake for 30 minutes.

Serves 6.

Cheese Lover's Chicken Casserole

1 large chicken
2 cans condensed cheddar
   cheese soup
1 can condensed cream of
   mushroom or cream of
   celery soup
1 1/2 cups celery, finely chopped
1/2 cup onion, finely chopped
2 cans (4 oz. each) green
   chiles, chopped

1 jar (4 oz.) mushroom pieces
   (optional)
1/4 cup chicken broth
1/2 lb. cheddar cheese, grated
   (optional)
1 pkg. (2 oz.) potato chips,
   crushed
1/4 lb. butter

Simmer the chicken whole with onion, celery, salt, and pepper for seasoning. Cool and remove meat from the bones in large pieces.

Preheat oven to 375 degrees.

Pour 1 can of cheddar cheese soup into a 9×12-inch casserole. Place the chicken pieces evenly over the soup layer. Cover with the cream of mushroom soup. Mix the celery, onions, green chiles, and mushrooms. Spoon evenly over the mushroom soup.

Cover with the second can of cheddar cheese soup diluted slightly with 1/4 cup chicken broth. Sprinkle the grated cheese on top.

Bake for 30 minutes. Remove from the oven. Increase the temperature to 400 degrees. Cover the casserole with potato chips and dot generously with butter. Bake an additional 10 minutes or until the casserole is golden brown.

Serves 6.

Family Chicken 'n Chile Casserole

1 can condensed cream of chicken
  soup
1 can condensed cream of
  mushroom soup
1 cup chicken broth or milk
1 can (4 oz.) sliced mushrooms,
  undrained

1 cup green chiles, chopped,
  or chile salsa or chile
  relish
2 cups cooked chicken or
  turkey, cubed
12 corn tortillas
1 cup onions, chopped
1 cup cheese, grated

Preheat oven to 350 degrees.

Mix together the soups, broth or milk, mushrooms, chiles, and chicken.

Lightly fry the tortillas in oil. Drain. Line a 9×13-baking dish with half the tortillas. Add half the chicken-soup mixture, half the onions, and half the cheese.

Repeat the layers, ending with the cheese. Bake for 30 minutes. Serves 6.

Variation—Add 1 cup of sour cream to the soup mixture.

Variation—Omit the cream of mushroom soup and grated cheese. Stir 1 jar (8 oz.) processed cheese spread into the soup mixture.

Variation—Omit the corn tortillas and layer the chicken and sauce with 1 pkg. (9 oz.) corn chips or tortilla chips.

Variation—Omit the chicken from the soup mixture. Omit the onions and grated cheese from the recipe. Add $1/2$ cup dry sherry to the sauce and pour over the baking chicken pieces. Bake, uncovered, 20 minutes longer.

Crabmeat Pudding

1 Tbs. butter
1 Tbs. flour
1/4 tsp. salt
1 cup milk
1 can (7 3/4 oz.) crabmeat

1 cup green chiles, chopped
2 cups fresh corn or 1
 can (16 oz.) whole
 kernel corn, drained
1 egg, lightly beaten

Preheat oven to 350 degrees.

Melt the butter and add the flour and salt; blend together and add the milk. Stir until the milk is scalded. Add the crabmeat, green chiles, and corn. Stir in the lightly beaten egg.

Butter a 9-inch square baking dish and pour the mixture into it. Sprinkle with pepper. Dot with butter and bake for 30 minutes.

Serves 6.

Fish 'n Chile

1 lb. flounder or sole fillets,
 thawed
1 egg
1 cup cracker crumbs

1 cup green chiles, chopped
1 cup cream of celery soup
1/4 cup water

Preheat oven to 375 degrees.

Divide the thawed fish and cut it into 12 strips. Place the fish, egg, and cracker crumbs in a mixing bowl. Coat the fish with crumbs and egg.

Butter or grease a muffin pan. Arrange the fish fillets around the outer edges of the muffin pockets and place chiles in the center of each fish muffin.

Bake 15 minutes. Cool 5 minutes. Remove from the pan and place in a 12×7 1/2-inch baking dish.

Dilute the cream of celery soup with 1/4 cup water and pour it over the fish. Return the fish to the oven and bake 5 minutes more.

Serves 4 to 6.

Fiesta Casserole

1 can (9 1/4 oz.) tuna
1 can condensed cream of
    mushroom soup
1 soup can water or milk
1 medium onion, chopped
3 stalks celery, chopped
1 can (8 oz.) corn
1 tsp. garlic powder
1 tsp. salt

1 tsp. coarsely ground black
    pepper
1 pkg. (12 oz.) egg noodles
1/4 lb. mushrooms
1 Tbs. butter or margarine
8 whole green chiles,
    peeled
1 pkg. (8 oz.) cheddar cheese,
    sliced

Preheat oven to 375 degrees.

Combine the tuna, mushroom soup, water or milk, onion, celery, corn, garlic powder, salt, and pepper in a saucepan. Heat the mixture to a boil; then remove from heat.

Cook the noodles according to the package directions.

Sauté the mushrooms in butter until lightly browned.

In a casserole, layer the egg noodles, then tuna, then green chiles, then 4 slices of cheese. Repeat. With the mushrooms, form a circle on top and place the remaining cheese in circle. Bake 30 to 40 minutes. Excellent cold as well as hot.

Serves 6 to 8.

Variation—Substitute chicken for tuna.

Tuna à la Green Chile

1 medium onion, diced	1 can (6 oz.) tomato paste
3 green chiles, diced	2 cans (8 oz. each) tomato
$1/4$ tsp. pepper	sauce
$1/4$ tsp. salt	1 can ($6^1/2$ oz.) tuna
1 clove garlic, sliced	1 Tbs. wine vinegar
1 Tbs. oil	10 oz. rigatoni or spaghetti

Place the first 6 ingredients in a saucepan and brown, about 10 minutes. Add the tomato paste and tomato sauce and cook another 5 minutes. Add the tuna and vinegar and simmer. Cook the pasta according to the package directions. Toss the cooked pasta with the tuna mixture.

Serves 4.

Lamb Roast with Green Chile

4 lbs. lamb roast (loin, shoulder, or half leg)	6 slices uncooked bacon
2 cloves garlic, finely chopped	1 can (10 oz.) tomatoes with green chiles
2 cans (4 oz. each) whole green chiles, roasted and peeled	

Preheat oven to 325 degrees.

Score the fat side of the lamb roast and press garlic pieces into the meat. Spread the whole green chiles over the roast, letting them hang down over the sides and end of the meat. Place the bacon slices over the green chiles. Insert a meat thermometer and place the roast on a rack in a roaster, chile side up. Pour the can of tomatoes with green chiles over the entire roast.

Cover and cook 4 hours or to 180 degrees on the meat thermometer. Baste several times with the drippings. Uncover the roast the last 30 minutes to crisp the bacon. Let the roast stand 15 minutes before carving. Serve lamb slices with bacon and green chiles.

Serves 10.

Pork Loin in Green Sauce

4 lbs. lean pork, boneless
1 onion, chopped
1 bay leaf

1/8 tsp. marjoram
1/8 tsp. thyme
2 tsp. salt

SAUCE:

1 onion, quartered
1 clove garlic
1 cup tomatillos (or green
    tomato relish)
1 large tomato, peeled and
    quartered

3 canned green chiles
    (or more to taste)
2 Tbs. cooking oil
2 Tbs. cilantro, chopped
    (or parsley)
1 cup broth from meat
Salt and pepper to taste

Cover the meat with cold water. Add the onion, bay leaf, marjoram, and thyme. Cook, covered, 3 hours. Add the salt after 1 1/2 hours.

Purée the onion, garlic, tomatillos, tomato, and chiles. Fry the paste in hot oil for 5 minutes. Stir in the cilantro and broth; salt and pepper to taste.

Slice the meat, add it to the sauce, and simmer 30 minutes. Serve with hot rice or boiled potatoes.

Serves 8.

Italian Green Chile Casserole

1 lb. Italian sausage, sliced
   and browned
1 clove garlic, minced
1 Tbs. onion, chopped
1 sweet basil leaf
1 Tbs. parsley, chopped
$^1/_4$ tsp. cayenne pepper
$^1/_4$ tsp. oregano

3 cups green chiles, chopped
$1^1/_2$ cups pinto beans, cooked
$^1/_2$ tsp. salt
2 cups water
$^1/_4$ tsp. black pepper
1 can (6 oz.) tomato paste
1 can (16 oz.) tomatoes

Combine all the ingredients and cook for 30 minutes. Serve over Cornmeal Mush.

Serves 4 to 6.

CORNMEAL MUSH:

1 cup cornmeal
1 cup cold water

3 cups boiling water
$1^1/_2$ tsp. salt

Mix the cornmeal with the cold water and add the boiling water and salt. Cook over medium heat 7 to 10 minutes, stirring occasionally.

Chile-Sausage Sauté

6 Italian sausages, halved and
   skins removed
1 can (16 oz.) whole tomatoes

8 to 10 large green chiles,
   peeled
Salt and pepper to taste

Place the sausages in a large skillet with water to half cover them. Heat to moderate and boil until all the water has been evaporated. Continue cooking until the sausages are brown on all sides.

Cool slightly; then lay the chiles on top of the sausages and add the tomatoes. Do not stir. Cover and cook over low heat for 15 minutes. Uncover and cook to desired consistency. Season with salt and pepper to taste.

Serves 4.

Stuffed Hard Rolls

12 hard rolls
1/2 lb. ham or Spam, cubed
1/2 lb. longhorn cheese, cubed
1 can (8 oz.) black olives, chopped
1 can (4 oz.) green chiles, chopped
6 green onions, chopped
1 can (8 oz.) tomato sauce
1/4 cup salad oil
3 hard-cooked eggs, chopped
1/2 tsp. salt
Dash garlic salt

Preheat oven to 350 degrees.
Slice the rolls in half and scoop out the soft centers.
Mix 1 cup of the crumbs with all the other ingredients. Stuff the mixture into the rolls and wrap each in aluminum foil. Bake for 30 minutes.
Makes 12.

Chile Dogs in Blankets

8 hot dogs
8 strips American cheese
1 can (4 oz.) green chiles, chopped
1 can (8 oz.) refrigerated crescent rolls

Slit the hot dogs lengthwise almost in half. Place a strip of cheese and 1 teaspoon of chopped chiles in each hot dog.
Roll each hot dog in a crescent roll and bake according to package directions.
Serves 4.

Variation—Wrap filled hot dogs in corn tortillas. Brown in hot oil until they are crisp and the cheese is melted.

Veal Parmigiana à la New Mexico

1 lb. veal cutlets, thinly
    sliced (about 6)
1 egg, slightly beaten
3/4 cup fine dry seasoned
    bread crumbs
1/4 cup butter or margarine
1 jar (16 oz.) meatless
    spaghetti sauce

1 can (4 oz.) green chiles,
    chopped (or more, if
    desired)
8 oz. mozzarella cheese,
    sliced
1 can (4 oz.) mushrooms,
    drained
Parmesan cheese, grated

Preheat oven to 350 degrees.

Dip the veal cutlets first in egg and then coat them well with bread crumbs. Heat the butter in a skillet over moderately low heat; add the veal, increase temperature to moderately high, and brown the veal well on both sides.

Pour a layer of spaghetti sauce into the bottom of a shallow, 2-quart baking dish. Arrange the veal in a single layer over the sauce. Spread the green chiles evenly over the veal; then arrange the sliced mozzarella over chiles. Add the drained mushrooms to the remaining sauce and pour it over the cheese. Sprinkle generously with Parmesan cheese and bake 35 minutes.

Serve with additional grated Parmesan cheese, if desired.

Serves 4.

Vegetarian
Main Dishes

Monterey Jack Soufflé

12 slices bread
Soft butter or margarine
1 1/2 cups whole kernel corn
1 cup fresh chiles, peeled and
    cut into strips

2 cups Monterey Jack
    cheese, shredded
4 eggs, slightly beaten
3 cups milk
1 tsp. salt

Trim the crusts from the bread. Spread butter or margarine on the bread; then cut each slice in half. Arrange half the bread in a greased 3-quart casserole. Cover with half the corn. Place chile strips over the corn. Sprinkle with half the cheese. Repeat layers. Combine the eggs, milk, and salt and pour over the casserole. Cover and refrigerate 4 hours or longer.

Preheat oven to 350 degrees.

Bake for 45 to 50 minutes or until puffy and brown.

Serves 5 to 8.

Olive Lover's Cheese Entrée

12 corn tortillas, torn into
    strips
1/2 lb. Monterey Jack cheese,
    shredded
1/2 lb. sharp cheddar cheese
    shredded
2 cans (4 oz. each) green
    chiles, chopped

1 cup green olives, drained
    and sliced
6 eggs, beaten
1 tsp. dry mustard
4 cups milk
8 green stuffed olives,
    whole

Butter an 8×13-inch baking pan. Alternate layers of tortilla strips, cheese, chiles, and sliced green olives. Beat the eggs and combine them with the dry mustard and milk. Pour over the tortilla-cheese layers. Refrigerate for at least 1 hour or overnight.

Preheat oven to 350 degrees.

Bake for 1 hour. Garnish with whole stuffed olives before serving.

Serves 6 to 8.

Mexican Mix-Up

1 can (15 oz.) tamales, cut
   into bite-size pieces
1 can (15 oz.) chile with beans
1 can (4 oz.) green chiles

1 pkg. frozen whole kernel
   corn
1 can (16 oz.) tomatoes
Cheddar cheese, grated

In a large saucepan, combine all the ingredients except the cheese. Simmer, uncovered, for 25 to 30 minutes.

Serve in bowls topped with grated cheese.

Serves 4 to 6.

Meatless Lasagne

2 Tbs. cooking oil
1 large onion, chopped
1 clove garlic, minced
6 mushrooms, sliced
Green pepper, chopped
1 1/2 cups stewed tomatoes
1 can (1 lb.) kidney beans,
   drained (optional)
2 cans (4 oz. each) green
   chiles, chopped
1/2 cup dry red wine

1 Tbs. chile powder
1 tsp. ground cumin
Salt
6 to 8 corn tortillas
1/2 cup Monterey Jack cheese,
   grated
1/4 cup ricotta cheese
1/2 cup yogurt
1 can (8 oz.) pitted black
   olives

Preheat oven to 350 degrees.

Sauté the onion, garlic, mushrooms, and green pepper in the oil until soft. Add the tomatoes, beans, green chiles, wine, spices, and salt to taste. Simmer 30 minutes.

Combine the ricotta cheese and yogurt.

In a greased 3-quart casserole dish, layer the sauce, tortillas, cheese, and ricotta mixture. Repeat, ending with the sauce. Top with black olives. Bake 15 to 20 minutes or until bubbly.

Serves 5.

Company Casserole

4 Tbs. cooking oil
1 large onion, diced
1 medium bell pepper,
   finely chopped
1 can (16 oz.) tomatoes
1 can (10 oz.) tomatoes with
   green chiles

1 can (10 oz.) green chiles
   seeded and coarsely
   chopped
1 can (8 oz.) tomato sauce
12 corn tortillas
2 cups mild cheddar cheese,
   grated
1 cup sour cream

Preheat oven to 350 degrees.

In a large skillet sauté the onion and bell pepper in the cooking oil; add the next 4 ingredients and simmer 15 minutes.

Cut the tortillas into quarters and fry them lightly in hot oil. In a large casserole, place a layer of tortillas and top with part of the hot tomato and chile mixture. Sprinkle with part of the cheese. Repeat the layers and top with sour cream. Bake, covered, for 30 minutes.

Serves 8.

Variation—Omit the canned tomatoes and tomatoes with green chiles; instead, substitute 2 cans (7 oz. each) mild or hot taco sauce.

Variation—Omit the canned tomatoes and canned tomatoes with green chiles; instead, layer the other ingredients and top with 1 can condensed cream of chicken soup diluted with 1 soup can evaporated milk. Top with grated cheddar cheese and bake 1 hour at 325 degrees.

Spinach Quiche

2 pkgs. frozen spinach, chopped
2 Tbs. butter
1/2 cup onions, chopped
2/3 cup milk
4 eggs, slightly beaten
2 cups rice, pre-cooked
1/2 cup green chile, chopped

4 oz. cheese, grated
1/3 Tbs. salt
1/2 Tbs. rosemary
1/2 Tbs. thyme
1 Tbs. Worcestershire
   sauce

Cook the spinach according to package directions and drain.

In a large skillet, cook onion until transparent. Remove from heat; beat milk into eggs and add, with rice, chile, spinach, cheese, and eggs, salt, rosemary, thyme and Worcestershire sauce.

Bake in a shallow greased baking dish about 35 minutes or until set, in 350 degree oven.

Serves 6.

Chiles Rellenos Guillermos

10 whole green chiles, peeled
1/2 lb. Monterey Jack cheese,
   cut into 10 strips
1 cup cheddar cheese, grated
3 eggs
1/4 cup (scant) flour

3/4 cup milk
1/4 tsp. salt
Black pepper to taste
Dash of liquid hot pepper
   sauce

Preheat oven to 350 degrees.

Leave a few seeds in the green chiles for flavor. Spread the chiles on paper towels and pat dry. Slip a strip of Monterey Jack cheese in each chile and lay them side-by-side in a greased 9×13-inch baking dish. Sprinkle with cheddar cheese. Beat the eggs; add the flour, beating until smooth. Add the milk, salt, black pepper, and pepper sauce. Beat thoroughly. Carefully pour the egg mixture over the chiles. Bake, uncovered, for 45 minutes or until a knife inserted in the custard comes out clean. Freezes well.

Serves 4.

Green Chile Casserole

2 cans (4 oz. each) whole
   green chiles
$1/2$ lb. longhorn cheese, grated
2 eggs
$1/2$ cup evaporated milk

Sprinkle of garlic salt and
   paprika
$1/2$ lb. mozzarella cheese,
   grated
1 can condensed cream of
   chicken soup

Preheat oven to 350 degrees.

Stuff the green chiles with the longhorn cheese, reserving some for garnish; place them in a greased 9×13-inch baking dish, side-by-side. Beat the eggs with the milk. Add the garlic salt and mozzarella. Pour the mixture over the chiles. Spread the cream of chicken soup over the top and sprinkle the remaining longhorn cheese on it. Add paprika for color. Bake for 45 minutes or until set.

Serves 4 to 6.

Easy Relleno Bake

1 cup (or about 10 oz.) whole
   green chiles
$1^1/2$ cups Monterey Jack
   cheese, grated
$1^1/2$ cups longhorn cheese,
   grated

4 eggs, separated
$3/4$ tsp. baking powder
3 Tbs. flour
3 Tbs. cornmeal
$1/4$ tsp. salt

Preheat oven to 325 degrees.

Slit the chiles open and, if desired, remove the seeds and veins.

Mix the cheeses together and reserve $1/4$ cup. Shape the cheese mixture to fit inside chiles. Put the cheese in the chiles and close the slits. Place the chiles in a buttered 10×6×2-inch baking dish, seams down.

Beat the egg whites until stiff and set aside; then beat the egg yolks well. Blend the dry ingredients and add to the yolks, mixing well; fold in the egg whites.

Pour the batter over the chiles and sprinkle with the remaining $1/4$ cup cheese. Bake 15 to 20 minutes or until lightly browned on top.

Serves 3 to 4.

Quick Chile-Corn Chip Casserole

8 eggs, separated
5 tsp. flour
1^1/$_2$ tsp. salt
1^1/$_2$ tsp. instant minced garlic
1 tsp. crushed oregano
1 tsp. red chile powder

1 lb. Monterey Jack cheese,
  sliced
1^1/$_2$ cups green chiles,
  chopped
3 Tbs. sunflower seeds,
  roasted and salted
3 Tbs. corn chips, crushed

Preheat oven to 325 degrees.

Beat the egg yolks with the flour, salt, garlic, oregano, and chile powder. Whip the egg whites very stiff and fold the yolk mixture into the whites. Spread half of this mixture in a greased 2-quart casserole dish and cover it with half of the sliced cheese, then all of the green chiles. Lay the remaining cheese over the chiles and cover completely with the remaining egg mixture. Sprinkle with the sunflower seeds and crushed corn chips. Bake for 25 to 30 minutes or until the top is golden brown and the center is just firm.

Serves 6.

Rellenos on Spanish Rice

2 cans (16 oz. each) stewed
   tomatoes
1 medium green pepper, diced
2 slices cooked bacon,
   crumbled
1 1/2 tsp. salt
1/2 tsp. oregano
1/4 tsp. pepper
1 1/2 cups quick cooking rice

6 green chiles, roasted
   and peeled
6 oz. Monterey Jack or
   cheddar cheese, cut
   into 6 strips
1/3 cup pancake mix
1/2 tsp. onion powder
1/2 tsp. paprika
1/4 cup hot water

Preheat oven to 325 degrees.

Mix the first 7 ingredients in a 1 1/2-quart greased casserole. Cover and bake for 1 hour. Stuff the green chiles with the strips of cheese. Remove the casserole from the oven and gently push the stuffed chiles halfway into the Spanish rice. Mix together the remaining ingredients and spread the batter over the top of the green chiles. Increase the oven temperature to 400 degrees and bake, uncovered, for 30 minutes or until browned.

Serves 6.

Relleno Bean Bake

1 can (16 oz.) refried beans
1 medium onion, diced
3 medium tomatoes, peeled
   and chopped
1/2 tsp. salt
1/4 tsp. garlic powder
6 green chiles, roasted
   and peeled

6 oz. Monterey Jack cheese
   or cheddar cheese,
   cut into 6 strips
1/3 cup pancake mix
1/2 tsp. onion powder
1/2 tsp. paprika
1/4 cup hot water

Preheat oven to 400 degrees.

Evenly layer a 1 1/2-quart greased casserole with the first 5 ingredients in the order listed. Stuff the cheese into the green chiles and arrange in a row as the next casserole layer. Push the chiles slightly down into the beans. Mix the dry ingredients together, add hot water, and stir. Spread over the green chiles. Bake for 30 minutes or until browned. Remove from the oven and let sit for 10 minutes.

Serves 6.

f f f

Do-Ahead Chile Sourdough Casserole

*4 to 6 slices sourdough
French bread
2 to 3 Tbs. soft butter
2 cups cheddar cheese,
shredded
2 cups Monterey Jack
cheese, shredded
1 can (4 oz.) green chiles,
chopped*

*6 eggs
2 cups milk
2 tsp. salt
2 tsp. paprika
1 tsp. crumbled oregano
$^1/_2$ tsp. pepper
$^1/_2$ tsp. dry mustard
$^1/_4$ tsp. garlic powder*

Cut the bread into $^1/_2$-inch-thick slices and remove the crusts. Butter one side of each slice. Arrange in a $7^1/_2 \times 11^1/_2$-inch baking dish with the buttered sides down. Sprinkle the cheddar cheese evenly over the bread; then sprinkle the Monterey Jack cheese evenly over the cheddar. Scatter green chiles over the cheeses. Beat the eggs until well blended; then add the milk and seasonings and beat again. Pour the egg mixture over the cheeses and chiles. Cover and chill overnight.

Bake at 350 degrees for 45 to 50 minutes or until lightly browned. Let stand for 10 minutes before cutting into squares. Serve with hot Enchilada Sauce, on next page.

Serves 6.

Enchilada Sauce

2 Tbs. butter

2 Tbs. flour

3¹/₂ tsp. chile powder

1 tsp. cumin

1¹/₂ tsp. garlic salt

¹/₂ tsp. garlic powder

1 can (6 oz.) tomato paste

2¹/₄ cups milk

Make a roux of the butter and flour. Add the spices and tomato paste. Stir until well blended. Gradually add the milk, stirring constantly until well blended. Heat until hot. Serve over squares of Do-Ahead Chile Relleno Casserole.

Makes 4 cups.

Sopaipillas Rellenas

1¹/₂ lbs. green chiles

2 tsp. salt

Garlic to taste

1 qt. cooked pinto beans

6 sopaipillas

1 Tbs. lard or oil

6 oz. American cheese, grated

1 small onion, chopped

1 small head lettuce, chopped

2 tomatoes, chopped

Peel and chop the green chiles. Season with the salt and garlic to taste. Mash the pinto beans and fry them in lard or oil with the cheese and onion, stirring frequently for 10 minutes.

Add the green chiles. Cut the sopaipillas on one end and fill them with the chile-bean mixture. Add the chopped lettuce. Garnish with tomatoes.

Serves 6.

Green Chile Quiche

1 can (8 oz.) refrigerated
  crescent rolls
2 cans (4 oz. each) whole
  green chiles
1 cup Monterey Jack cheese,
  cubed

3 large eggs, beaten
3 Tbs. milk
$1/2$ tsp. salt
Dash bottled hot pepper sauce
2 tsp. parsley, chopped

Preheat oven to 325 degrees.

Separate the crescent roll dough into 8 triangles. Place in an ungreased 8- or 9-inch pie pan, pressing pieces together to form a crust. Seal well.

Cover the bottom of the crust with green chiles. Place the cheese on top of the chiles.

Mix the eggs, milk, seasonings, and parsley together and pour over the top. Bake for 45 to 50 minutes or until the edges are golden brown.

Serves 6 as an entrée or 12 as an appetizer.

Swiss Chard Pie

1 small onion, chopped
$1/4$ cup butter or margarine
30 leaves Swiss chard, torn
  into pieces

2 eggs, slightly beaten
$1/3$ cup green chiles, chopped
$1/2$ cup cheese, grated

Preheat oven to 350 degrees.

Sauté the onion in butter until transparent. Add the chard and cook 1 minute or until the chard wilts. Be sure the chard is covered with butter.

Pour into a pie pan. Mix the eggs with green chiles and pour over the chard. Stir around with a fork.

Sprinkle cheese on top and bake until firm.

Serves 6 to 8.

Cheese and Chile Pie

3/4 cup sharp cheddar cheese, grated

1/4 cup onion, finely chopped

3 slices bacon, cooked crisply and crumbled, or 1/4 lb. bulk sausage, browned

1 can (4 oz.) green chiles, chopped

1 9-inch pie shell, baked

3 eggs, beaten

1/2 cup cream or evaporated milk

1/4 tsp. salt

1/8 tsp. pepper

1 1/2 Tbs. butter or margarine

Preheat oven to 375 degrees.

Mix the cheese, onion, bacon, and green chiles. Spread in the bottom of a pie shell. Mix the eggs and cream with salt and pepper. Pour over the cheese mixture. Dot the top with butter. Bake 40 minutes.

Serves 4 as an entrée or 6 as an appetizer.

Tortillas Malibu

1 small onion, chopped

2 Tbs. butter

1/2 cup fresh mushrooms, chopped

2 cups frozen whole kernel corn

3/4 cup sour cream

3 large green chiles, chopped

6 corn tortillas

Sauté the onion in butter until soft; add the fresh mushrooms and corn; simmer 6 minutes. Then add the sour cream and chopped green chiles; simmer 3 minutes, stirring constantly.

Fry the tortillas until crisp; spread them with the sour cream mixture and serve immediately. A good sangría goes beautifully with this dish.

Serves 6.

Mesa Verde Maíz

2 cups prepared pancake
   batter
1 cup cheddar cheese, grated
1 pkg. frozen whole kernel
   corn

1 can (4 oz.) green chiles,
   chopped
1 can (15 oz.) tomatoes with
   green chiles

Preheat griddle.

Mix the pancake batter with cheese, corn, and green chiles. Fry like pancakes. Top them with tomatoes and green chiles.

Serves 6 to 8.

Green Chile Pizza

1 pkg. dry yeast
$^3/_4$ cup lukewarm water
$2^1/_2$ cups biscuit mix
Parmesan cheese, grated
1 can (8 oz.) tomato sauce

1 lb. longhorn cheese, grated
1 can (4 oz.) green chiles,
   chopped
1 lb. mozzarella cheese, grated
Oregano

Preheat oven to 400 degrees.

Dissolve the yeast in warm water. Stir in the biscuit mix. Beat 20 times. Put on a well-floured breadboard and knead 20 times. Divide the dough in half for 2 medium-size pizzas or leave it whole for 1 large pizza. Roll the dough thin and place it on a pizza pan. Sprinkle with the Parmesan cheese. Pour on the tomato sauce. Sprinkle with the longhorn cheese. Spread the chopped chiles over cheese. Then put on a layer of mozzarella. Top with Parmesan cheese and the oregano. Bake 20 minutes. Freezes well.

Serves 8.

California Casserole

1 cup onions, chopped
1/4 cup butter or margarine
4 cups cooked rice
2 cups sour cream
1 cup cream-style cottage
   cheese
1 large bay leaf

1/2 tsp. salt
1/8 tsp. pepper
3 cans (4 oz. each) green
   chiles, drained
2 cups sharp cheddar
   cheese, grated
Parsley, chopped

Preheat oven to 375 degrees.

Sauté the onions in the butter until golden. Remove from the heat and stir in rice, sour cream, cottage cheese, bay leaf, salt, and pepper. Lightly mix. Layer half the rice mixture in a buttered baking dish. Cover with half the chiles and sprinkle with 1 cup of the cheddar cheese. Repeat. Bake 30 minutes. Sprinkle with chopped parsley.

Serves 8.

Accompaniments

Palma's Chile Antipasto

20 chile peppers, roasted and
    peeled
2 jars (4 oz. each) pimentos, cut
    into strips
3 Tbs. black olives, chopped
1/4 cup olive oil
1/4 tsp. black pepper

1/4 tsp. garlic powder or
    3 cloves garlic
1/4 tsp. salt, or to taste
1/2 tsp. oregano
1 tsp. parsley flakes
1 Tbs. lemon juice

Combine all the ingredients in a bowl.

Toss them gently together, mixing well. Serve at room temperature
with French or Italian bread and cold cuts.

Serves 4.

Green Chile Salad Dressing

4 cloves garlic
2 jars (4 oz. each) pimentos
5 green chiles

1 jar (10 oz.) chile sauce
1 qt. salad dressing

Mix the garlic, pimentos, and chiles and chop very fine. Add the
chile sauce and salad dressing and mix all the ingredients well. Chill.
Serve on green salads or hard-boiled egg sandwiches.

Makes 1 3/4 quarts.

Pickled Green Chile

1/2 cup vinegar
1/2 cup sugar
1 tsp. salt
1 tsp. dill seed
1/2 tsp. mustard seed
Salt to Taste

2 1/2 cups green chiles,
    chopped, or 1 1/2 cups
    green chiles, cut into
    strips
Garlic

Combine the vinegar, sugar, and spices and simmer for 5 minutes.
Pack the chiles into small jars, cover with syrup, and add a piece of
garlic to all jars. Cover tightly and refrigerate for 3 days before using.
Makes 2 1/2 pints.

Green Pepper-Green Chile Marinade

3 green bell peppers, sliced
3 or 4 green chiles, sliced
1/8 cup olive oil

1/8 cup vinegar
Garlic salt to taste

Stir all the ingredients together in a saucepan and cook, covered,
over medium to low heat until the flavors are combined. Also good as a
side dish.
Serves 3 to 4.

Orange Jalapeño Pickles

2 cups fresh cucumbers,
  peeled and finely chopped
2/3 cup sweet red peppers,
  finely chopped
2/3 cup jalapeño chiles,
  finely chopped
2 Tbs. salt

1/4 cup cold water
1 1/2 oranges
1 cup vinegar
1 cup brown sugar
1/2 tsp. mustard seed
1/2 tsp. celery seed

Combine the cucumbers, red peppers, and jalapeño chiles with salt and water and let stand overnight. In the morning drain the vegetables and discard the liquid.

Squeeze the oranges and save the juice for drinking; grind the orange pulp and peel in a blender or food grinder.

Combine the orange mixture with the vegetables and remaining ingredients and bring it to a boil; cook 25 minutes.

Pack in hot, sterilized jars; seal at once. Process in boiling water bath (212 degrees) for 10 minutes.

Makes 1 1/2 pints.

Chile Verde en Escabeche

30 lbs. fresh green chiles,
  roasted and peeled
6 small cloves garlic
4 onions, sliced
4 cups corn oil

1 small bay leaf to each pint
1/8 tsp. oregano to each pint
4 Tbs. salt
6 cups white vinegar
5 cups hot water

Remove the stems from the chiles and leave whole. Fry the garlic and onions in oil until limp; add all the spices. Add the vinegar and water in which salt has been dissolved. Bring to a boil and add the chiles. Fill jars and seal.

Makes 10 pints.

Million Dollar Chile Relish

8 cups cucumbers
4 cups green chiles
2 green bell peppers
3 large onions
3 carrots
1 jar (2 oz.) pimentos

$^1/_2$ cup pickling salt
5 cups white sugar
1 tsp. salt
1 tsp. turmeric
1 Tbs. mustard seed
$2^1/_2$ cups white vinegar

Grind the vegetables medium coarse. Sprinkle them with $^1/_2$ cup pickling salt, cover with cold water, and let stand for 3 hours. Drain thoroughly. Combine the sugar, salt, tumeric, and mustard seed in a kettle. Add the cucumber-chile mixture to the spices and cover with the vinegar. Boil until the vegetables are tender, about 10 minutes.

Pour into hot sterilized jars and seal.

Makes 8 or 9 pints.

Sour Cream Relish

1 pt. sour cream or sour half-
    and-half
1 can (4 oz.) green chiles,
    chopped

1 medium onion, finely
    chopped
$^1/_2$ tsp. garlic salt

Mix all the ingredients together. Chill several hours. Serve as a relish or dip.

Serves 12.

Yugoslavian Eggplant Relish

2 medium-size eggplants,
  stems removed
2 Tbs. olive oil
2 green peppers
2 large tomatoes
4 cloves garlic, minced

2 cans (4 oz. each) green
  chiles, chopped
2 tsp. salt
$1/2$ tsp. pepper
4 Tbs. olive oil
2 Tbs. red wine vinegar

Cut the eggplants in half lengthwise. Rub the cut surfaces with 2 tablespoons olive oil. Cut the green peppers in half and remove the seeds. Place the eggplants and peppers, cut sides down, on a rimmed pan and bake in a 400-degree oven for about 45 minutes or until eggplants are very soft and the skins of the peppers are charred.

Cool the vegetables slightly; then with the fingers pull the peels from the eggplants and green peppers; coarsely chop the vegetables and combine them in a bowl with the remaining ingredients.

Stir to blend, cover, and chill for at least 2 hours or as long as overnight.

This relish is delicious served with grilled meats.

Makes about 8 cups.

Sandwich Spread

1 can (13 oz.) evaporated milk
1 lb. cheddar cheese, grated
1 can (4 oz.) pimentos,
  chopped

1 can (4 oz.) green chiles,
  chopped

Combine the milk and cheese in a double boiler over hot water. Stir until the cheese melts and add the remaining ingredients.

Using a mixer, beat until smooth and well blended.

Good as a sandwich spread or for stuffing celery to make small canapes.

Makes 1 quart.

Pimento Cheese Spread

1 lb. American cheese, grated
1 pkg. (3 oz.) cream cheese
1 can (2 oz.) pimentos,
    chopped
$^1/_2$ cup green chiles,
    chopped, or to taste

$^1/_4$ cup pecans, finely
    chopped
$^1/_2$ cup mayonnaise or
    salad dressing

    Mix the ingredients in the order listed with the mayonnaise or salad dressing to the desired consistency. Also good with crackers.
    Serves 6 to 8.

Green Chile Sandwich Spread

1 pkg. (8 oz.) cream cheese,
    softened
1 can (4 oz.) green chiles,
    chopped
1 clove garlic, finely chopped

1 Tbs. Worcestershire
    sauce
$^1/_2$ cup salad dressing
2 Tbs. dried onions
Pepper and liquid hot pepper
    sauce to taste

    Combine all the ingredients. Spread on crackers, dark or regular rye, or on white bread.
    Makes 2 cups or 8 servings.

Green Chile Tortilla Sandwich

TORTILLAS:

4 cups flour

2 tsp. salt

2 tsp. baking powder

4 Tbs. shortening

1¹/₂ cups warm water

Heat griddle to 350 degrees.

With a pastry blender, mix together the first 3 ingredients. Cut the shortening into the mixture; then add warm water. Mix thoroughly with the hands to form a ball. Knead approximately 20 times; then let the dough rest for about 10 minutes. Form the dough into 9 balls and roll out. Place each on the griddle and cook 4 to 5 minutes on one side. Turn the tortilla; cook about 1 minute longer.

FILLING:

4 cups green chiles, roasted,
    peeled, and chopped

2 medium tomatoes, chopped

¹/₈ tsp. garlic salt

Salt to taste

2 Tbs. bacon bits

2 cups cheddar cheese,
    grated

Preheat oven to 450 degrees.

Combine the first 4 ingredients. Fold each tortilla in half and spread each with some of the above mixture. Sprinkle the tops with bacon bits and grated cheese. Heat until cheese is melted.

Makes 9.

Chile Verde
(Green Chile Sauce)

1 cup onion, chopped
3 cloves garlic, chopped
3 Tbs. oil
$^1/_2$ tsp. ground cumin

12 New Mexican green chiles,
   roasted, peeled, seeded,
   and chopped
$1^3/_4$ cups water

Sauté the onion and garlic in the oil until soft. Stir in the remaining ingredients, bring to a boil, and reduce to a simmer. Cook 30 minutes.

Makes 3 cups.

Variation—For a smooth sauce, purée in a blender.

Variation—Add 2 medium tomatoes, chopped.

❜ ❜ ❜

Mother's Chile Sauce

40 to 45 tomatoes, peeled and
   quartered
4 hot green chiles
4 large red bell peppers
9 large green bell peppers
9 large onions

6 cups sugar
2 qts. cider vinegar
1 tsp. cloves
6 Tbs. salt
1 tsp. chile powder
1 tsp. cinnamon

Grind the first 5 ingredients coarsely. Add the remaining ingredients and boil, stirring occasionally, until thick, about 3 or 4 hours. Pour into sterilized jars and seal tightly. Good with pot roast and meat loaf.

Makes 21 pints.

Fresh Chile-Tomato Sauce

16 fresh green chiles,
    roasted, peeled, and
    chopped
1/4 tsp. garlic salt
1/2 tsp. salt
1 lb. lean ground beef
2 Tbs. shortening

1/4 cup onions, chopped
2 1/2 Tbs. flour
1 can (16 oz.) whole peeled
    tomatoes
2 1/2 cups water
6 jalapeño chiles, diced
    (optional)

In a medium bowl, mix the green chiles with the garlic salt and salt; set aside.

In a skillet brown the ground beef; drain off the fat. In a separate pan sauté the onions in the shortening. When slightly browned, add the flour and make a smooth paste. Gradually stir in the canned tomatoes, the green chile mixture, and the 2 1/2 cups water. Stir in the browned beef and simmer for 5 minutes. (Diced jalapeños should be added if an especially hot mixture is desired.)

May be used as a sauce for tacos, enchiladas, or burritos or may be eaten in bowls by itself as a fiery entrée.

Serves 6.

Chile-Cheese Sauce

2 lbs. processed cheese
    spread
1 can (13 oz.) evaporated milk

1/2 cup green chiles,
    chopped
1 can (1 lb.) tomatoes

Melt the cheese spread and evaporated milk together in the top of a double boiler. Add the chopped chiles and tomatoes and stir thoroughly. Store in the refrigerator.

Great on green beans or other vegetables. Or it can be served cold as a fresh vegetable dip.

Makes 7 cups.

Salsa Macho con Tequila

12 green chiles, roasted,
  peeled, and chopped
6 green onions, chopped
1/2 medium onion, chopped
1 clove garlic, crushed
4 tomatoes, peeled and
  chopped

6 sprigs fresh cilantro
  (coriander), chopped
1 Tbs. salt
1 Tbs. wine vinegar
1 Tbs. salad oil
1 jigger (1 1/2 oz.) tequila

Mix all the ingredients in a large bowl, stirring together by hand. Add 1 cup water if a thinner mixture is desired.

Refrigerate at least 2 hours before serving.

Serves 8.

Green 'n Gold Salad

1 lb. cheddar cheese, grated
2 medium tomatoes, diced
1 small onion, chopped
2 medium avocados, diced or
  mashed

Juice of 1 lemon
1/8 tsp. garlic powder
1/8 tsp. salt
3 Tbs. mayonnaise
6 green chiles, peeled
  and sliced

Combine all the ingredients in the order listed.

Serves 5 to 6.

Green Chile Wine

1 lb. green chiles, peeled and
    seeds removed
3 lbs. sugar
1 gal. water
1 bisulfite tablet
3 yeast nutrient tablets
$^{1}/_{4}$ tsp. grape tannin

1 oz. acid blend
24 dried apricot halves
$^{1}/_{2}$ cup raisins, coarsely
    chopped
1 packet all-purpose wine
    yeast

Chop the green chiles into $^{1}/_{4}$-inch squares. Dissolve the sugar in very warm water. Crush the bisulfite and yeast nutrient tablets into a powder.

Mix together all the ingredients except the wine yeast in a 5-gallon polythene bucket. Cover with plastic wrap. This mixture is called the must.

When the must has cooled to 70 to 75 degrees, sprinkle the yeast on top. Cover bucket. Stir the must daily. Ferment for 5 days.

Strain out the solids and press the leftover pulp. Discard the pulp. Syphon the must into a narrow-necked 1-gallon jug or carboy. Cover with a double layer of plastic wrap secured with a rubber band or attach a fermentation lock.

Be sure the liquid is "topped" by adding water to bring the level within 1 inch of the top of the jug. Place the jug away from drafts of extreme temperature changes.

After 3 weeks, syphon the wine into a 5-gallon bucket, leaving as much of the yeast deposit behind as possible. Carefully rinse the jug and syphon the wine back into the the jug. Top the liquid again. Replace the cover. This process is called racking.

After 3 months repeat the racking process.

When the wine is clear and bubbles can no longer be seen rising in the liquid, bottle the wine. If corks are used, store the bottles on their sides. If screw caps are used, store upright.

Age 1 year before drinking. Makes 5 fifths of a dry wine with a distinctive green chile flavor.

Sweets

Apple Dessert Soufflé

4¹/₂ Tbs. quick-cooking
    tapioca
¹/₈ tsp. salt
1 cup milk, scalded
¹/₃ cup sugar
3 egg yolks, well beaten
¹/₂ Tbs. lemon juice

¹/₂ cup raw apple, grated
¹/₂ cup fresh green chiles,
    grated
3 egg whites, stiffly beaten
¹/₄ cup orange liqueur, warmed
2 cups whipped cream,
    sweetened

Preheat oven to 350 degrees.

Mix the tapioca with the salt and milk in the top of a double boiler; cook 15 minutes or until the tapioca is clear. Stir frequently. Add the sugar and cool.

Stir the beaten egg yolks, lemon juice, apple, and chiles into the cooked mixture; mix well. Fold in the beaten egg whites.

Bake for 1 hour in a greased baking dish placed in a pan of hot water.

When the soufflé is removed from oven, pour on the warmed orange liqueur. Top with the whipped cream and serve immediately.

Serves 8.

Jalapeño Jelly

3 large bell peppers, chopped
  in blender
6 medium jalapeños, chopped
  in blender
1¹/2 cups apple cider vinegar

6¹/2 cups sugar
1 bottle liquid pectin
3 to 4 drops green food
  coloring

Combine the bell peppers, jalapeños, vinegar, and sugar in a large saucepan and mix well. Bring to a full boil and boil for 8 or 9 minutes, stirring constantly.

Remove from the heat and add the pectin and food coloring. Mix well.

Return to the heat and boil for 2 minutes.

Remove from the heat, skim, and ladle into hot sterilized jars; seal at once.

Process in a boiling water bath (212 degrees) for 10 minutes.

Great served with cheese and crackers.

Makes 2¹/2 pints.

Jalapeño Candy

8 oz. Philadelphia Cream Cheese
1 drop jalapeño juice or powder

Red or green food
coloring

Beat the cream cheese until smooth. Add the jalapeño juice or powder and food coloring, mixing well. Add enough powdered sugar to make cookie dough consistency. Mold or flatten into mint size pieces. Let candies air a bit, then stack and store.

Serves 4.

Preparing Fresh Green Chiles

Fresh green chiles need to be peeled before being used. After rinsing and draining chiles, make a steam vent in each by using a toothpick or an ice pick.

Roasted or Broiled Chiles

1. ROAST them on your charcoal grill. Or BROIL them on a cookie sheet 2 to 6 inches below the broiler unit, leaving oven door open. Or ROAST them on a heavy wire mesh placed over a stovetop burner.

2. Turn them often so that they blister evenly all over. DO NOT BURN CHILES—they will be almost impossible to peel if allowed to blacken.

3. For crisp green chiles, plunge them into ice water after roasting/broiling. For a more cooked flavor, place them in a bowl and cover it with a cold damp towel to steam for 10 minutes.

Pan-Broiled Chiles

Brown them on all sides, then cover the pan with a wet cloth and let the pod steam for 10 minutes.

Peeling

To remove the tough outer skin, start at the stem end and peel downward. For rellenos (stuffed chiles), be sure to leave the stem end intact. For other dishes, you may wish to remove the stem and seeds at this stage.

Freezing

Chiles may be frozen whole without being peeled. The skins slip off quite easily when the chiles are thawed. In preparing chopped chiles for freezing, first peel them and remove the seeds and stems.

Where to Buy Chiles

The chile products used in these recipes are widely available in supermarkets and specialty stores in major metropolitan areas around the country. If you have difficulty finding chiles in your locality, call one of these reliable sources. Many of them provide regular mail order services.

SOUTHWEST

Bueno Foods
2001 4th Street SW
Albuquerque, NM 87102
505-243-2722
1-800-95CHILE
www.buenofoods.com

Casados Farms
Box 852
San Juan Pueblo, NM 87566
505-852-2433

Chile Addict
325 Eubank NE
Albuquerque, NM 87123
505-237-9070
www.chileaddictstore.com

The Chile Shop
109 East Water Street
Santa Fe, NM 87501
505-983-6080
www.thechileshop.com

Chile Traditions
8204 Montgomery Blvd. NE
Albuquerque, NM 87109
505-888-3166
1-877-VERY-HOT
www.chiletraditions.com

Los Chileros
401 2nd. St. S.W.
Albuquerque, NM 87102
505-768-1100
1-888-328-2445
www.888eatchile.com

Chili Pepper Emporium
901 Rio Grande NW
Suite A-194
Albuquerque, NM 87104
505-881-9225
1-800-288-9648
www.chilipepperemporium.com

Da Gift Basket
P.O. Box 2085
Los Lunas, NM 87031
505-865-3645
1-877-468-2444
www.dagiftbasket.com

Graves Farm & Garden
6265 Graves Road
Roswell, NM 88203
505-622-1889
rgraves@dfn.com

Hatch Chile Express
P.O. Box 350
Hatch, NM 87937
505-267-3226
1-800-292-4454
www.hatch-chile.com

Hobson Gardens
3656 Hobson Road
Rosell, NM 88203
505-622-7289
Seasonal operation

Jane Butel's Cooking School Pantry
Jane Butel's Pecos Valley Spice Co.
2655 Pan American NE
Albuquerque, NM 87017
505-243-2622
www.janebutel.com
www.pecosvalley.com

NM Chili.Com
2315 Hendola NE
Albuquerque, NM 87110
1-888-336-4228
www.nmchili.com
wholesale:
www.wholesalechili.com

Pendery's
1221 Manufacturing Street
Dallas, Texas 75207
1-800-533-1870
www.penderys.com

Santa Fe Chile Co.
500 Sandoval
Santa Fe, NM 87501
505-995-9667
www.chileco.com

Santa Fe School of Cooking
116 West San Francisco Street
Santa Fe, NM 87501
505-983-4511
www.santafeschoolofcooking.com

WEST & NORTHWEST

Casa Lucas Market
2934 Twenty-Fourth Street
San Francisco, CA 94110
415-826-4334

La Palma
2884 Twenty-Fourth Street
San Francisco, CA 94110
415-647-1500
fax: 415-647-1710

EAST

The Hot Shoppe
311 S. Clinton St.
Syracuse NY 13202
1-888-468-3287 (HOTEATS)
www.hotshoppe.com

Mo Hotta–Mo Betta
P.O. Box 1026
Savannah, GA 31402
1-800-462-3220
www.mohotta.com

Glossary of New Mexican Foods

Albóndigas—Meat balls.

Arroz con Polla—Chicken with rice.

Biscochitos—Anise seed cookies.

Burrito—Flour tortilla filled with refried beans and chile sauce, ground beef and chile sauce, or a combination of both and rolled.

Caldillo—Stew made of ground beef, raw potatoes, and seasoning.

Carne Adovada—Pork steak marinated in chile sauce, then roasted or pan fried. Usually served with Spanish rice and refried beans.

Chicarrones (Cracklings)—Pieces of fat cooked slowly until the lard is rendered out. Lightly salted, they may be served as a warm of cold hors d'oeuvre.

Chicos—Dried sweet corn used whole or crushed in a seasoned stew.

Chilaquilar—Corn tortillas sliced in strips and fried with onions, tomatoes, and cheese.

Chile Caribe—Red chile pods blended with water to a purée and seasoned. (Used in marinated meat dishes.)

Chile con Queso—Melted cheese dip seasoned with chile and served with tostados.

Chile Rellenos—Green chiles stuffed with cheese or meat and dipped in a corn meal batter and deep-fat fried.

Chiles, Green—Found in a variety of sizes, shapes, and piquancies, they are an important part of New Mexican dishes. Before use the skin is removed. Used in sauces, relishes, stews, and as chile rellenos.

Chiles, Red—Green chile that has ripened and dried. Usually used ground or crushed for added seasoning or in making a variety of sauces.

Chorizo—Highly seasoned hot link sausage.

Empanada—Fried or baked turnover with either dried fruit or sweet meat filling.

Enchilada—Rolled or flat corn tortillas topped or stuffed with meat, cheese, onion, and red or green chile sauce.

Enchilada Sauce—Red sauce made of mild to hot chile pulp or chile powder, spices, and beef or pork or both. Also called red chile sauce.

Flan—Caramelized custard.

Frijoles—Beans. Most commonly used bean is the pinto bean.

Frijoles Refritos—Refried beans. Pinto beans that have been boiled, mashed, fried in pork fat, and topped with longhorn or jack cheese.

Gazpacho—A cold vegetable soup with a meat broth or tomato juice base containing a variety of raw vegetables.

Guacamole—Avocado salad served as a dip or on lettuce as a salad, or ingredient in many other dishes.

Harina—All-purpose flour.

Harina Azul—Blue cornmeal flour for tortillas.

Huevos Rancheros—Fried eggs on a corn tortilla and topped with a special green chile sauce with onions and tomatoes. Served in several other ways, sometimes served with red or green enchilada sauce and garnished with lettuce and cheese.

Maíz—Corn.

Masa—A moist dough of ground, dried corn that has been soaked in limewater, then cooked. Used in tamales.

Menudo—Tripe and hominy, traditionally served on Christmas or New Year's Eve.

Nachos—An hors d'oeuvre of tostados topped with jack cheese, sour cream, and jalapeño chile.

Natillas—Soft custard topped with egg white and sprinkled with cinnamon.

Paella—A classic dish combining rice and a variety of both meat and seafood.

Piñon—Pine nuts (seeds) from piñon cones. Used in desserts and breads or roasted and enjoyed as nut meats.

Posole—Hominy stew made with dried lime-treated corn and combined with pork and seasonings.

Salsa Jalapeño—A hot sauce or relish made of jalapeño chiles, onions,
either red or green tomatoes, and seasonings.

Sopaipilla—Puffy, crisp, deep-fried bread. Accompanies many New
Mexican meals or may be stuffed with refritos or meat and topped
with chile sauce, cheese, and lettuce.

Taco—A corn tortilla folded in half and fried until crisp and stuffed
with meat, chicken, or refried beans. Before being served it is
topped with lettuce, onion, cheese, and taco sauce.

Tamale—Red chile and ground pork encased in fresh masa and
wrapped in a corn shuck. Usually steamed and served with red chile
sauce.

Tostada—Open-faced taco.

Tostados—Corn tortillas cut in pieces, fried until crisp, and salted
or sprinkled with chile powder. Served for dipping with salsa,
guacamole, or chile con queso.

Recipe List

Accompaniments

Appetizers

Breads, Rice, and Pasta

Breakfast

Angi's Potluck Eggs, 18
Baked Eggs with Cheese and Chile, 17
Chil-Ome, 19
Chile Breakfast Whirls, 14
Chile-Cheese-Sausage Pancakes or Waffles, 21
Chiles con Huevos, 15
Egg and Chile Omelet, 19
Green Chile Scrambled Eggs, 22
Huevos y Chilaquiles, 14
Huevos Yucatecos, 16
"I Can't Stand Eggs", 17
Mexican Omelet, 18
Salsa para Huevos Rancheros, 20
Sunday Grits, 20

Main Dishes with Meat

Anglo-Style "Carnitas", 110
Big Wheel Chile Burger, 99
Cheese Lover's Chicken Casserole, 120
Chicken Breasts Sauterne with Chile and Avocado , 114
Chicken Mexicana, 112
Chicken-Tomato Casserole, 119
Chicken with Pumpkin Seed Sauce, 113
Chile Dogs in Blankets, 127
Chile-Sausage Sauté, 126
Chile Stew Enchiladas, 101
Cottage Enchiladas, 102
Crabmeat Pudding, 122
Crusted Green Chile Loaf, 100
Family Chicken 'n Chile Casserole, 121
Fiesta Casserole, 123
Fish 'n Chile, 122
Gourmet Enchilada Parmesan, 117
Great Green Bean Chile, 97
Great Green Chile Casserole, 105

Salads

Soups and Stews

Sweets

Traditional Favorites

Sour Cream Enchiladas, 88
Sour Cream Enchiladas in a Stack, 90
Sweet Chile Albóndigas, 86
Taco Tempters, 88

Vegetables

Broccoli-Green Chile Delight, 64
Calabacitas Zowie, 77
Cauliflower-Chile Soufflé, 65
Chile-Mushroom Fritters, 78
Chile Scalloped Potatoes, 71
Corn and Green Chile, 67
Cornfetti Casserole, 66
Creamy Corn Casserole, 65
Creamy Vegetable Mélange, 76
Curried Corn with Chile, 66
Eggplant Olé, 67
Foil-Baked Chile Potatoes, 71
Garbanzos Calientes, 70
Green Beans with Green Chile, 68
Green Beans Supreme, 68
Green Chile-Mashed Potatoes, 72
Hominy and Green Chile Casserole, 69
Low-Calorie Delight, 75
Mexicali Spuds, 70
New Mexico Caviar, 69
Roundup Mashed Potatoes, 72
Southwest Baked Beans, 64
Southwestern Spinach, 73
Stuffed Zucchini, 74
Summer Squash Bake, 74
Zucchini Españolas, 73
Zucchini Esquibel, 76

Vegetarian Main Dishes

SOUTHWEST COOKBOOKS FROM CLEAR LIGHT PUBLISHING

"MUST-HAVE" BOOKS FOR CHILE LOVERS

RED CHILE BIBLE
Southwestern Classic & Gourmet Recipes

By Kathleen Hansel & Audrey Jenkins

"The definitive source of information on cooking with chile peppers." (Wichita Falls *Times Record News*)

This collection celebrates Spanish, Indian and Western traditions, covering the gamut from traditional to contemporary and from comfortably mellow to fiery hot, even including desserts (red chile cheesecake is hot stuff!)

ISBN 0940666936
168 pp., 6 x 9 (paperback) $12.95

GREEN CHILE BIBLE
Award-Winning New Mexico Recipes

Compiled & Edited by the Albuquerque Tribune

"This indeed is a bible for those who have become helpless addicts to green chile." (*New Mexico Magazine*)

This collection of 200 prize-winning recipes, from the traditional to the exotic, is a treasury of arguably the best green chile recipes in the world.

ISBN 0940666359
176 pp., 6 x 9 (paperback) $12.95

RED OR GREEN
New Mexico Cuisine

By Clyde Casey

"Red or Green?" This is the most commonly asked question in New Mexican restaurants. In *Red or Green: New Mexico Cuisine*, Clyde Casey helps you answer that question. He presents over 200 traditional and modern New Mexican dishes, from classic enchiladas to blue cornmeal pancakes with green chile chutney. Delicious ways to prepare fish and wild game as well as holiday recipes add to the eclectic mix. Also includes New Mexico wines and high altitude instructions. A perfect companion to the best-selling Clear Light titles *Green Chile Bible* and *Red Chile Bible*.

ISBN: 1574160907
272 pp., 6 x 9 (paperback) $14.95

For complete selection of all our titles, visit our web site at www.clearlightbooks.com

SOUTHWEST COOKBOOKS FROM CLEAR LIGHT PUBLISHING

BY THE AUTHORS OF *RED CHILE BIBLE*

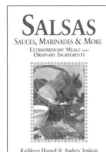

SALSAS, SAUCES, MARINADES & MORE
Extraordinary Meals from Ordinary Ingredients

By Kathleen Hansel & Audrey Jenkins

The authors of *Red Chile Bible* present an inspired selection of over 150 blends that will add flair, variety and zest to daily meals and party dishes, including a dazzling variety of sauces, dressings, glazes, rubs and marinades. They also include instructions on how to use these in the cooking process to add flavor and your own gourmet touch.

ISBN 1574160389
200 pp., 6 x 9 (paperback) $14.95

FIESTAS FOR FOUR SEASONS
Southwest Entertaining with Jane Butel

By Jane Butel, Photographs by Marcia Keegan

"Full of great menu ideas and recipes featuring South-west recipes...." **(Wichita Falls *Times Record News*)**

Beautifully illustrated with color photographs, this cookbook presents full menu ideas corresponding to the four seasons as well as an overview of the basics of Southwestern cooking.

ISBN 0940666723
35 color photos,192 pp., 8 x 8 (paperback) $14.95

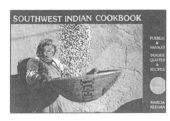

SOUTHWEST INDIAN COOKBOOK
Pueblo & Navajo Images, Quotes & Recipes

Edited and Photographed by Marcia Keegan

"Recipes, striking color photographs and an informative and beguiling text on the food and folklore...[A] loving and poetic presentation of both the cuisines and the people behind them." **(New York Times)**

Winner of the
R. T. French
Tastemaker
Award

"An amazing mix of history, folklore, photography and recipes from the American Southwest. ...An excellent addition to any cook's library." **(New England Review of Books)**

ISBN 0940666030
44 color photos,120 pp., 9 x 6 (paperback) $12.95

For complete selection of all our titles, visit our web site at www.clearlightbooks.com

MORE GREAT COOKBOOKS FROM CLEAR LIGHT PUBLISHING

GOURMET TORTILLAS
Exotic & Traditional Tortilla Dishes

By Karen Howarth

This cookbook shows how to make tortillas flavored and enhanced with a wide variety of surprising additions. It also offers recipes for main dishes from the traditional to the exotic. Great creative fun for all, from kids to gourmet cooks!

ISBN 1574160583
176 pp., 8 x 9¼ (paperback) $14.95

BREADMAKER'S GUIDE
Savory & Sweet Recipes from Around the World

By Jan Thomson

This treasury of instruction, recipes and practical wisdom offers recipes and practical wisdom for every level of expertise, as well as recipes for no-knead yeasted batter bread and alterations for bread machines. An essential addition to the kitchen bookshelf.

ISBN 1574160494
296 pp., 6 x 9 (paperback) $14.95

SOUPS, STEWS & QUICKBREADS
495 Quick & Easy Recipes from Around the World

By Jan Thomson

*"A cornucopia of imaginative, nutritious, attractive easy gourmet recipes that will delight the eye as they please the palate." (**Bookwatch**)*

A lifesaver for the busy cook, this book offers hundreds of quick, light and hearty "meals in a bowl" and a nearly endless choice of breads to be served on the side.

ISBN 1574160028
222 pp., 6 x 9 (paperback) $14.95

For complete selection of all our titles, visit our web site at www.clearlightbooks.com

MORE GREAT COOKBOOKS FROM CLEAR LIGHT PUBLISHING

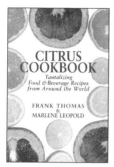

CITRUS COOKBOOK
Tantalizing Food & Beverage Recipes from Around the World

By Frank Thomas & Marlene Leopold

This collection of over 200 recipes, featuring citrus fruits or flavoring, offers everything from variations on standards to mouth-watering originals, including appetizers, salsas, beverages, soups, sauces, dressings, meats, seafood and desserts.

ISBN 1574160567
160 pp., 6 x 9 (paperback) $14.95

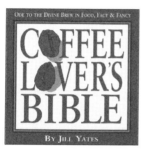

COFFEE LOVER'S BIBLE
Ode to the Divine Brew in Food, Fact & Fancy

By Jill Yates

"All you need to know about coffee and many varieties of hot and cold drinks, plus fantastic desserts." (**Eagle-Tribune Lifestyle**)

This enjoyable volume provides 101 recipes for drinks to desserts to savory main dishes as well as all the tips you need from selecting beans to brewing that perfect cup of coffee. With delightful old-style illustrations and quotes.

ISBN 1574160141
Illustrations, 208 pp., 7½ x 7½ (paperback) $12.95

HAPPY CAMPER'S COOKBOOK
Eating Well Is Portable™

By Marilyn Abraham & Sandy MacGregor

"A handy cookbook and charming travel guide based on their experiences living and cooking in a recreational vehicle." (**Albuquerque Journal**) *"These recipes are quick, simple and fun. The advice on everything from grilling to gazpacho is perfect."* (**Jessica Harris, author of** The Africa Cookbook)

The easy and tasty recipes and techniques can be used in the home as well, especially on the backyard grill.

ISBN 1574160249
125 recipes, 40 Illustrations, 144 pp., 6 x 9 (paperback) $14.95

For complete selection of all our titles, visit our web site at www.clearlightbooks.com

ORDER FORM

I WANT TO PURCHASE THE FOLLOWING TITLES:

TITLE	PRICE	QTY	TOTAL
Green Chile Bible	*$12.95*		
Red Chile Bible	*$12.95*		
Red or Green: New Mexico Cuisine	*$14.95*		
Southwest Indian Cookbook	*$12.95*		
Fiesta for Four Seasons	*$14.95*		
Salsas, Sauces, Marinades & More	*$14.95*		
Gourmet Tortillas	*$14.95*		
Citrus Cookbook	*$14.95*		
Coffee Lovers Bible	*$12.95*		
Happy Camper's Cookbook	*$14.95*		

See more titles at our on-line catalog www.clearlightbooks.com/cookbook

SUBTOTAL	
PLEASE ADD: 1st Copy UPS Shipping & Handling $4.00	
Each Additional Copy 50¢	
NM Residents Add 7.625% Sales Tax	
TOTAL	

SHIP TO:

Name _____ _____ Phone _____

E-mail Address _____

Address _____

Address Line 2 _____

City _____ State _____ Zip _____

COMPLETE CATALOG AVAILABLE ON-LINE
www.clearlightbooks.com

VISA and MasterCard accepted
Call 1-800-253-2747 for credit card orders
e-mail: order@clearlightbooks.com
823 Don Diego • Santa Fe • New Mexico • 87505
(505) 989-9590 • Fax: (505) 989-9519

This order form may be photocopied & mailed or faxed.
Shipping charges and sales tax rates subject to change.